Undisciplined

America and the Long 19th Century

GENERAL EDITORS
David Kazanjian, Elizabeth McHenry, and Priscilla Wald

Black Frankenstein: The Making of an American Metaphor
Elizabeth Young

Neither Fugitive nor Free: Atlantic Slavery, Freedom Suits, and the Legal Culture of Travel
Edlie L. Wong

Shadowing the White Man's Burden: U.S. Imperialism and the Problem of the Color Line
Gretchen Murphy

Bodies of Reform: The Rhetoric of Character in Gilded-Age America
James B. Salazar

Empire's Proxy: American Literature and U.S. Imperialism in the Philippines
Meg Wesling

Sites Unseen: Architecture, Race, and American Literature
William A. Gleason

Racial Innocence: Performing American Childhood from Slavery to Civil Rights
Robin Bernstein

American Arabesque: Arabs and Islam in the Nineteenth Century Imaginary
Jacob Rama Berman

Racial Indigestion: Eating Bodies in the Nineteenth Century
Kyla Wazana Tompkins

Idle Threats: Men and the Limits of Productivity in Nineteenth-Century America
Andrew Lyndon Knighton

Undisciplined

*Science, Ethnography, and Personhood
in the Americas, 1830–1940*

Nihad M. Farooq

NEW YORK UNIVERSITY PRESS
New York

NEW YORK UNIVERSITY PRESS
New York
www.nyupress.org

Portions of chapter 1 appeared in "Narrating Sense, Ordering Nature: Darwin's Anthropological Vision," *Concentric: Literary & Cultural Studies* 38, no. 2 (2012): 87–111. © 2012 Department of English, National Taiwan Normal University. All rights reserved. Reprinted by permission. Portions of chapter 3 appeared in "Creolizing Cultures: Franz Boas, Zora Neale Hurston, and Ethnographic Performance in the Twentieth Century," *Studies in the Humanities* 41, nos. 1, 2 (2015). © 2015 Nihad M. Farooq. An earlier version of chapter 4 appeared as "National Myths, Resistant Persons: Ethnographic Fictions of Haiti," in *Journal of Transnational American Studies* 5, no. 1 (2013): 1–36. © 2013 Nihad M. Farooq.

LIBRARY OF CONGRESS CATALOGING-IN-PUBLICATION DATA
Library of Congress Cataloging-in-Publication Data
Names: Farooq, Nihad M., 1971– author.
Title: Undisciplined : science, ethnography, and personhood in the Americas, 1830–1940 / Nihad M. Farooq.
Description: New York : New York University Press, 2016. |
Series: America and the long 19th century | Includes bibliographical references and index.
Identifiers: LCCN 2015049159 | ISBN 9781479812684 (cl : alk. paper) | ISBN 9781479806997 (pb : alk. paper)
Subjects: LCSH: Ethnology—America—History—19th century. | Ethnology—America—History—20th century. | Philosophical anthropology—History—19th century. | Philosophical anthropology—History—20th century. | Persons—Philosophy.
Classification: LCC E29.A1 .F37 2016 | DDC 305.80097—dc23
LC record available at http://lccn.loc.gov/2015049159 References to Internet websites (URLs) were accurate at the time of writing.

Neither the author nor New York University Press is responsible for URLs that may have expired or changed since the manuscript was prepared.

New York University Press books are printed on acid-free paper, and their binding materials are chosen for strength and durability. We strive to use environmentally responsible suppliers and materials to the greatest extent possible in publishing our books.

Manufactured in the United States of America

10 9 8 7 6 5 4 3 2 1

Also available as an ebook

A book in the American Literatures Initiative (ALI), a collaborative publishing project of NYU Press, Fordham University Press, Rutgers University Press, Temple University Press, and the University of Virginia Press. The Initiative is supported by The Andrew W. Mellon Foundation. For more information, please visit www.americanliteratures.org.

THE
AMERICAN
LITERATURES
INITIATIVE

For my Todd,
for our families,
and for all who have journeyed from elsewhere

Contents

Acknowledgments

This book is about journeys—from chance adventures to forced relocations, wanderings to willful missions—that foster new bonds of community and kinship, sometimes among the most seemingly disparate groups of people. Such encounters and travels in my own life—some difficult, most serendipitous—have helped me forge a rich and unexpectedly diverse network of family and friends, mentors and colleagues, who have shaped the ideas and spirit that guides this work. I could not have written a single word without their profound gifts of time, empathy, and love that I believe are foundational to productive intellectual thought.

Early research for this book began in the Darwin Archive of the Cambridge University Library. I am thankful to Adam Perkins and the librarians who facilitated my research there, and for the Georgia Tech Research Foundation for making that visit possible. I am grateful to the librarians at the Newberry Library in Chicago for their research funding and assistance as well. This project could not have come to fruition without additional grants and research support from the Dean's Office of Ivan Allen College at Georgia Tech; and the generous support of the Andrew W. Mellon Foundation, and the Robert Penn Warren Center for the Humanities at Vanderbilt University.

I am so grateful to the anonymous reviewers who read early versions of these chapters, and who devoted significant time, energy, and care to encourage and strengthen this work. My special thanks, also, to the series and production editors from NYU Press, including Tim Roberts and Susan Murray, for the indexing services of Martin L. White, and for the kindness and dedication of Eric Zinner and Alicia Nadkarni, who believed in this project from the start.

For their mentorship, friendship, and support in my years at Georgia Tech, I owe a tremendous debt of gratitude to Ron Broglio, Hugh Crawford, Lauren Curtright, Angela Dalle Vacche, Shannon Dobranski, Fox Harrell, Karen Head, Jillann Hertel, Liz Hutter, Wes Kirkbride, Ken

Knoespel, Michelle Miles, Vinicius Navarro, J. C. Reilly, Jackie Royster, Aaron Santesso, Carol Senf, Jay Telotte, Nirmal Trivedi, Richard Utz, Sneha Veeragoudar-Harrell, Qi Wang, Lisa Yaszek, and Greg Zinman. Special thanks, in particular, is due to Laura Bier, Carol Colatrella, Elizabeth Freudenthal, Narin Hassan, Lauren Klein, Janet Murray, and Anne Pollock, for reading earlier versions and chapters of this manuscript, and many other pieces of writing along the way. For keeping us all organized and sane year after year, I am grateful for the kindness, professionalism, and dedication of Kenya Devalia, Dawn Jackson, Jocelyn Thomas, Grantley Bailey, and Melanie Richard. And for keeping me both grounded and on my toes each day, I am grateful for my smart, humble, and always-inspiring students, who are a daily reminder of the myriad ways in which our ideas and research are nourished.

I am grateful to have had such a productive research year at the Robert Penn Warren Center for the Humanities at Vanderbilt University in 2012–13. Although our Sawyer Seminar had a thematically foundational impact on my *next* project, it also played a significant role in helping me to expand and finalize this one. For their incredible gifts of generosity, kindness, good humor, and intellect during that memorable year, I offer my sincerest thanks to Mona Frederick, Allison Thompson, Hillary Pate, and our fantastic seminar group, Emily August, Caree Banton, Richard Blackett, Celso Castilho, Teresa Goddu, Jane Landers, Herbert Marbury, Catherine Molineux, Daniel Sharfstein, and the many other faculty members and guests with whom I was fortunate to share my ideas, especially Colin Dayan, Anna Everett, and Maria Helena Pereira Toledo Machado, who all helped to solidify these ideas, and to coax new ones.

Along this way have been teachers and mentors aplenty: Srinivas Aravamudan, Adrian Bailey, Mary Baine Campbell, Bill Cook, Wai Chee Dimock, Tom Ferraro, Ronald Green, Ranji Khanna, Deborah King, Tom King, Tom Luxon, Pat McKee, Don Pease, Kathy Psomiades, Cannon Schmitt, and Ivy Schweitzer were all among my earliest interlocutors during my undergraduate and graduate years. Houston Baker, Cathy Davidson, and Priscilla Wald are not only three of the most brilliant intellectuals with whom I have had the privilege to work but are three of the most humble and generous individuals I have had the great fortune to know. I owe the greatest debt to my advisor, Priscilla Wald, whose unwavering support and genuine commitment to ideas and people make her a sterling example of the kind of scholar and teacher so many of us aspire to be.

In his desire to foster the lonely intellectual he knew lurked beneath my extroverted spirit (and also to keep the phone lines open), my father always advised me, in my teen years: "Don't pick up that phone—pick up a book instead!" All these years later, I am still as likely to do the former as the latter, and for that, I have been rewarded with the blessings of friendships that have imbued my life and work with joy, texture, and an increasingly important sense of history: Kathy Fidler, Kristen (Nordt) Franklin, Dan Garodnick, Chad Kessler, Virginia Lanigan, Margaret Laurence, and Christine Svitila know me better than most, and are foundational to my very self. I could not have survived graduate school and beyond without the friendship and intellectual energy of Monique Allewaert, Max Brzezinski, Katey Castellano, Lauren Coats, Kate Crassons, Melinda DiStefano, Joseph Fitzpatrick, Erica Fretwell, Anne Gulick, Sarah Harlan, Cara Hersh, Jenny Hubbard, Casey Jarrin, Jaya Kasibhatla, Stacy Lavin, Monu Lahiri, Vin Nardizzi, Eden Osucha, LaTarsha Pough, Britt Rusert, Amardeep Singh, and Jini Watson. And for those who have made Atlanta less solitary over these many years and chapters, I owe a special thanks to Warner Belanger, Munia Bhaumik, Danielle Bobker, Emily Brock, Natalia Cecire, Ann Claycombe, Elena Conis, Rena Diamond, Javier Garcia, Rebecca Hill, Danny LaChance, Matt Lasner, Dawn Peterson, Justin Remais, Jenny Rhee, Lauren Ristvet, Esra Santesso, Jake Selwood, Michele Reid Vazquez, Trish Ventura, and Nick Wilding—many of whom have also read parts of this, offered generous feedback, and shared their own work, ideas, and dear friendship, too.

All of the people listed on these pages are present somewhere in this book, kindred spirits without whom words, ideas, and passion would not be possible for me. But the ones who are present, in every thought and in each breath, are my immediate kin: parents, siblings, grandparents, aunts, uncles, and cousins, whose love and prayers from around the world have supported me at every stage and through every milestone. I owe thanks to each of them, and especially to my parents, Dr. Faheem and Mariam Farooq, who have devoted their lives and their journeys to saving mine from the day it began. They have modeled for me, through their incomparable gifts of strength, affection, wisdom, courage, and sacrifice, what a true labor of love really is. There are no words to express the blessings of such a boundless love, and the infinite grace it inspires. Every word, every smile, and every success in this life is for them and because of them. And finally, I thank the stars for my dear Todd, whose capacious intellect, adventurous spirit, generous heart, and wondrous way of examining and navigating this world remind me of some of the wanderers who roam these chapters, and whose depth and presence (editorial and inspirational) I feel on every page, and in every journey we are blessed to share together.

Undisciplined

Introduction

> The relentless search for the purity of origins is a voyage not of
> discovery but of erasure.
>
> Joseph Roach, *Cities of the Dead*

Darwin and the Middle Passage

In the spring of 1836, in the waning months of a five-year, global expedition, the HMS *Beagle*, carrying the young but now-seasoned naturalist Charles Darwin, rounded the Cape of Good Hope and reentered the
South Atlantic, en route to its home port of Falmouth, England. However,
the ship's temperamental captain, Robert FitzRoy, ordered a detour back
along the Brazilian coastline, to reconfirm measurements he had taken
in the ship's earlier visit to Salvador at the start of their voyage in 1832.
With its exhausted crew in tow, the HMS *Beagle* thus crossed the Atlantic
from Africa back to Brazil, before heading home to Falmouth—a triangular path common to European traders and traffickers in human flesh for
centuries, as part of the Middle Passage.[1] The convergence of science and
the triangle trade in Atlantic spaces was hardly a new phenomenon in this
era. As scholars like Christopher Iannini, Londa Schiebinger, and others
have noted, "science traveled predominantly along trade routes" from the
eighteenth century onward, as European slave traders were also joined in
Atlantic waters by "colonial bioprospectors" who sailed through the New
World in search of botanical sources for medicine, food, and luxury goods
along these same routes.[2]

The crew of HMS *Beagle* was returning, however, from a very different, if parallel, kind of journey. As a survey barque of the Royal Navy, the
Beagle had already completed one hydrographic survey trip through the
Americas from 1826 to 1830, and had embarked on this, its second journey, in the fall of 1831. But hydrographic research was not the primary

aim of this second venture. Rather, it set out to conclude an earlier scientific experiment: the HMS *Beagle* was returning three captives from Tierra del Fuego that FitzRoy, erratic captain and copious "collector," had kidnapped during its first surveying voyage, in an act of ransom-turned-Christianizing mission.[3]

After spending nearly fourteen months in British custody, as neither enslaved laborers nor free colonial subjects but as objects of scientific and cultural curiosity, the three Fuegians (originally four in number—one had died of smallpox upon arrival in England) were sent back to their homeland, under the auspices of setting up a missionary settlement. FitzRoy had actually struggled for funding from the Royal Navy for this second trip. The Admiralty was not particularly keen on the Fuegian mission and also felt that further research in the southernmost Americas was unnecessary. But FitzRoy finally secured support for the return voyage, in part through the help of his well-connected uncle, the Duke of Grafton, and through Francis Beaufort, a friend and mentor in the Hydrographer's Office, who advocated for the modernization and colonial expansion of Britain through the merging of nautical and scientific exploration.[4]

Darwin's incidental appointment to this journey—based on FitzRoy's last-minute request for a scientific "traveling companion" (in part to keep him sane on a passage through this ominous portion of the New World that had led the *Beagle*'s previous captain to suicide)—and the subsequent birth of a theory that would fundamentally challenge perceptions of science and culture for centuries to come, was thus made possible, in part, by FitzRoy's spontaneous act of kidnapping and the necessity of the Fuegians' return—a significant recrossing which I will address at further length in chapter 1.

In the course of Darwin and Fitzroy's five-year journey aboard HMS *Beagle* from 1831 to 1836, the Atlantic became an increasingly complicated space for both colonists and captives alike. The British had passed the Slavery Abolition Act in 1833, which outlawed the practice of slavery throughout its empire. Darwin witnessed some of the changes prompted by the act, as he had contact with some mariners and other scientists (like astronomer John Herschel) in southern Africa who were there, in part, to ensure this empire-wide mandate.[5] During his stay here, as well as in St. Helena (where emancipation had actually been ongoing, in a phased process, since 1827, and where Chinese and Indian laborers were brought in to supplement the newly indentured workforce), Darwin—an abolitionist himself—commented on the recently emancipated slaves he saw, and how they seemed to "value fully" their freedom.⁶ This observation, of course, overlooked the fact that these emancipated persons were still bound to the land and to their former masters as indentured servants for at least another two years before they could count themselves as "free." And despite Britain's attempts to police the Atlantic waters, it had not managed to entirely abolish the trade or the practice of slavery. For from here, the *Beagle* continued west, crossing through the Middle Passage back into the Americas, where the trade in Brazil, and its practice, in the southern United States, continued to flourish.

As the ship traversed these Atlantic waters, portals of profound historic, economic, and cultural significance, Darwin's notebooks already contained, in great narrative detail, his varied encounters with the slave trade throughout his five-year journey. From his witness of trafficking (both legal and illegal) to his observations of emancipated and maroon communities; from the swift and desperate escape offered by slave suicide to the slow, gradual debasement of physical and emotional character that accompanied the cruelty of auctions and torture, Darwin's narrative journey is haunted, in part, by the practices, ghosts, and remnants of the Atlantic's most prosperous and horrifying business.

Darwin's earliest comments on slavery point to the cultural hypocrisy he saw as central to its practice. For example, on April 8, 1832, during his first visit to Brazil, Darwin wrote that as he and his party rode along granite hills from the village of Ithacaia to Lagoa Marica, they came upon a group of runaway slaves who often worked to "eke out a subsistence" in this area by "cultivating a little ground." However, they were soon discovered, and when a party of soldiers was sent, "the whole were seized with the exception of one woman, who, sooner than again be led into slavery, dashed herself to pieces from the summit of the mountain. *In a Roman matron this would have been called the noble love of freedom: in a poor negress it is mere brutal obstinacy.*"⁷

Darwin's antislavery remarks often relied on this relativistic comparison that sought to break down the socially constructed barriers between one group of humans and another. As the HMS *Beagle* pulled away from the Brazilian coast for the last time, Darwin began this long, passionate, and graphic diatribe, from which I offer a generous excerpt:

On the 19th of August we finally left the shores of Brazil. I thank God, I shall never again visit a slave-country. To this day, if I hear a distant scream, it recalls with painful vividness my feelings, when passing a house near Pernambuco . . . that some poor slave was being tortured, yet knew that I was as powerless as a child even to remonstrate. . . . Those who look tenderly at the slave-owner, and with a cold heart at the slave, never seem to put themselves into the position of the latter:—what a cheerless prospect, with not even a hope of change! Picture to yourself the chance, ever hanging over you, of your wife and your little children—those objects which nature urges even the slave to call his own—being torn from you and sold like beasts to the first bidder! And these deeds are done and palliated by men, who profess to love their neighbours as themselves, who believe in God, and pray that his Will be done on earth![8]

Darwin's sympathetic yet helpless stance performs quite keenly the conflicted nature of his personal sense of guilt about slavery. His words above are pleading and melodramatic, almost expiatory, turning on him even as they work, on the surface, to repress and assuage his guilt of voyeurism and cowardice in the face of violence, a guilt which is replayed in the act of confessing this encounter in writing. He begins by assuring readers that he will never, in fact, return to a slave country, distancing himself immediately from this practice, as well as these people (including the enslaved) as an outsider. Instead he admits his desire to repress the "painful vividness" he feels when any scream—of his own children in distress, perhaps—transports him back to a moment when he actually had an opportunity to help his fellow man: He passed by the home of suffering, in Pernambuco, where a slave was being tortured, and simply kept walking, insisting now that he was "powerless as a child even to remonstrate." It is here that his confession of cowardice turns upon itself, as Darwin now dons the role of priest, responding with shame that men (like himself) could "profess to love their neighbours as themselves," yet allow their fellow men ("even" the slave, whom *nature* has also endowed with a love for his own children) to be treated like beasts.

Darwin's prose often vacillates throughout his work between these modes of distance and proximity, of witness and mastery, as if the larger political implications of his realizations about kinship are, in fact, too much to bear. As an abolitionist and member of the egalitarian elite class, Darwin did distance himself from a practice that he found barbaric and inhumane. However, as a European scientist aboard a vessel that had just released its own captives to their native homeland, and in a moment in which the Atlantic began to emerge as a space where the lines between captivity and freedom, humanity and commodity, natural and cultured, native and migrant, became increasingly tenuous, Darwin's journey and research were deeply intertwined with the legacy of Atlantic exploitations; a legacy as foundational to the new era of science as he was.[9]

As Darwin returned to England in the fall of 1836 and settled into his life at Down House to ruminate upon his findings, Atlantic persons had already begun to change the landscape of the New World: In Haiti, a successful slave revolt in the final years of the last century had already challenged deterministic notions of Africans' so-called "natural" propensity for servitude and submission; the Native Baptists' Christmas Slave Revolt in Jamaica (which began just as the HMS *Beagle* set sail on its legendary second voyage), though unsuccessful in its immediate aims, was a key factor in the British abolition of slavery; and although the 1830s marked a new kind of bondage to the West with indentured servitude in the recently emancipated British colonies (and a recent reparations deal made with France that would carry Haiti into its subsequent political and economic crises), the Atlantic space began, ever so slightly, to shift, as the routes of some ships offered new possibilities: to life in emancipated colonies, to Africa, to a sea that was rife with political uncertainty. Ships, then, became more opportunistic spaces than they once were for Africans who had not long ago been immediately transformed into cargo by setting foot inside their holds. There was a burgeoning realization along the shoreline that one's status as *subject* or *object* was dependent on the permeable boundaries of conflicting nations and changing laws—clearly demarcated on land but murky in international waters. Movement offered a chance, for escape, and for reconstitution.

As anthropologist Michel-Rolph Trouillot famously noted, the Caribbean itself may have led the charge in these shifts in Atlantic space, as it had been an "undisciplined region" since Columbus landed there in 1492, refusing any categorization by Europeans to stand as its image of "the Savage Other." Trouillot explains that "the swift genocide of the aboriginal populations, the early integration of the region into the international circuit of capital, the forced migrations of enslaved Africans and indentured Asian laborers, and the abolition of slavery by emancipation or revolution all meant that the Caribbean would not conform with the emerging divisions of Western academia." Thus "the entire corpus of Caribbean cultural anthropology" can be read against this "basic incongruity between the traditional object of the discipline and the inescapable history of the region."[10]

My own title, *Undisciplined*, extends Trouillot's formulation, tracing such incongruities in Atlantic spaces between the objects and parameters of disciplinary thought itself, and the historical and social processes that challenge, destabilize, or unravel them. It pairs the drama, for example, of Darwin's transatlantic scientific journey that would eventually prove the speciousness of a hierarchical ordering of human beings (evolution), with the drama of economic and imperial enterprises built on that very premise of social hierarchy and purposeful design (colonization and slavery). I bring these stories together, performed as they are on the same stage, in order to add the magnifying lens of scientific inquiry to a critical examination of the Atlantic and the Americas first offered by scholars and writers like Paul Gilroy, Joseph Roach, Édouard Glissant, and James Clifford, and later honed by literary theorists like Sibylle Fischer and Laura Doyle.[11] These earlier interrogations have taken on the problematic myths of national, cultural, and racial origins, and have argued the importance, instead, of reimagining the transatlantic space as an intercultural network that cannot be grasped, as Fischer has argued, by "teleological narratives."[12]

This book contributes to these interrogations by using Darwin's own nonteleological narrative of human evolution—a narrative that emerged from his encounters with indigenous and enslaved American populations—as a starting point for reconsidering how Atlantic forms of personhood, culture, and nation continually disrupted European and Enlightenment categorizations. Darwin's 1831 journey and the subsequent scientific articulations it provoked in biology, anthropology, and ethnography inaugurated a literary, cultural, and political era that effectively unsilenced an already active resistance to the European romance of origins. Darwin's cautious title, *On the Origin of Species* (1859), in fact, belies his scientific narrative of a gradual, unceasing creolization.

The chapters that follow move through Darwin's century through the varied journeys and archives of transatlantic scientific and literary border-crossers—from Darwin, Louis Agassiz, William James, and Pauline Hopkins in the first half, to Franz Boas, Melville Herskovits, Zora Neale Hurston, Claude McKay, Langston Hughes, and Katherine Dunham in the second half. My emphasis, often on different kinds of writing or performance than that for which these particular figures are best known, also encourages a broader reading of how African American and Atlantic literature is counted as such, following in the spirit of scholars like Eric Gardner, whose urgent and astute remapping of the field of early

African American literature calls on readers to "broaden even further the list of authors and texts" that constitute this diverse canon.[13] Crucial to my own book's historical and generic frame is the formation, as well as the fault lines, of discrete disciplines in this period: the nascent fields of biology, anthropology, and psychology, tenuous and intertwined as they were, would offer theories that, in turn, modeled and mirrored the instability of other disciplinary categories like race and personhood. From notebooks to novels, letters to photographs, plays to dances, rituals to testimonies, the materials I use to investigate these fault lines themselves illustrate the overlapping terrains through which these ideas and disciplines traveled and unraveled.

When FitzRoy and Darwin returned to Tierra del Fuego in March 1834, thirteen months after depositing the three Fuegians in their homeland, they were astonished to find that their former charges had "reverted" back to their native way of life. Jemmy, York, and Fuegia (as these three persons had been renamed by FitzRoy and his crew) had abandoned the British customs they had so readily and successfully adopted during their brief stint abroad, and had fully reintegrated themselves back into Fuegian society.[14] For the Fuegians, this reassimilation marked their successful reentry into their home communities. For the British, it stood as a mark of atavism.

Although Darwin and FitzRoy's account (and the many that have followed, including my own) is admittedly a ventriloquized and limited filter for our knowledge of these three captive travelers, and while their true feelings will always remain unknowable, the record of subsequent encounters between the Britons and the Fuegians, especially with Jemmy, is particularly useful in our attempts to understand the malleability of cultural performance and the limits of interpretation, as I will discuss in more detail in chapter 1. In FitzRoy's account of his reunion with Jemmy, the young man is described as initially ashamed to see his British counterparts again, but he soon opens up, reassuring them of his contentment. When FitzRoy expresses concern at Jemmy's emaciated and unkempt appearance, the young Fuegian rejects this reading of his body, politely countering in English with the reassurance: "I am hearty, sir, never better. . . . Plenty fruits, plenty birdies, ten guanacoes in snow time, and too much fish."[15] When Jemmy later joins the captain for dinner aboard the *Beagle*, dressed and mannered as a proper Englishman, he assures his old British friend once again that "he did not wish to go back to England."

He then introduces his British peers to the person who FitzRoy and Darwin hypothesize might be at the root of "this great change" in Jemmy: "his young and nice-looking wife." FitzRoy's Fuegian experiment thus seems to serve as profound a cultural lesson for the Britons as it was for Jemmy Button. In fact, Darwin wonders aloud whether this journey of defamiliarization had instilled in Jemmy a stronger sense of patriotism than before, writing that "I do not now doubt that he will be as happy as, perhaps happier than, if he had never left his own country."[16]

Jemmy's sympathetic ability to read and reassure his British peers of his happiness and good health is not only a polite rejection of the British reading of his atavism but also a subtle but important example of the ways in which the studied subjects of scientific encounter worked to challenge the Enlightenment conception of self-determined personhood as a uniquely European trait. Neither Darwin nor FitzRoy could turn the Fuegians' choice into a narrative of inevitability and determinism. Jemmy, York, and Fuegia had readily adapted to English culture when forced to do so, and just as easily reacculturated themselves to their home environment when given the opportunity.

This episode, a precursor to others like it that I will address in the chapters to follow, marks a pivotal moment in the crossing of disciplines and persons in Atlantic spaces that would shape the century to come. Through his exposure to this single-generation cultural transformation of the Anglicized Fuegians and their unassimilated counterparts at home, coupled with the "new way of seeing" and writing that his landscape and experiences demanded, Darwin's journey through the Americas contributes to a burgeoning concept of cultural relativity, and bears witness to shifting practices of personhood in Atlantic spaces that would pave the way for a generation of others to link all humans "along the arc of culture."[17]

The narrative of the infamous second voyage of the *Beagle* and the tale of the three Fuegian travelers are by now well known. The effort to resituate Darwin's travels, writings, and theories within a broader literary, historical, and philosophical framework (by scholars like George Levine, Cannon Schmitt, and Elizabeth Grosz, among others) has brought increased attention to his influence on nineteenth-century culture, his own racial politics, and the contemporary feminist implications of natural selection.[18] Inspired by such cross-disciplinary investigations, I examine the ways in which the scientific and cultural entanglements of

Atlantic travelers in and beyond the Darwin era invite us to attend more closely to the consequences of mobility and migration on disciplines and persons.

New discourses and performances of personhood, culture, and nation emerged in the nineteenth century through these transatlantic crossings—of forced and voluntary migrations, and of scientific and colonial expeditions. Whether expressed as narratives of acculturation or as acts of resistance against the camera, the pen, or the shackle, the stories and assertions of the studied and stolen subjects of the Atlantic world add a new chapter to debates about personhood and disciplinarity in this era, in which biological and cultural kinship play a more dominant role in blurring the boundaries of racially determined personhood. These encounters and performances in Atlantic spaces—by observers and observed alike—also call for renewed attention to the creolization of the human sciences themselves, especially biology and anthropology, and the role they played—often in spite of their own purported aims—in challenging racial hierarchies.

Enlightenment discourse defined personhood in temporal and spatial terms of history and self-continuity. In John Locke's well-known formulation, the person is a "thinking, intelligent being, that has reason and reflection, and can consider itself as itself, the same thinking thing in different times and places."[19] Despite conditions and circumstances, the possession of self-consciousness over time and space was the constitutive mark of personhood, according to Lockean philosophy. Thus even the prince who changes bodies with the cobbler, yet carries in his consciousness the memory of his princely past is still a prince, "accountable only for the prince's actions."[20] By this extension, any embodied or material articulation of the prince—as animal, as machine, as oak tree—as long as it carries princely self-consciousness, may retain and claim his personhood as prince. But what happens to the princely self-consciousness in the slave body? Or in the body of an indigenous member of the Yamana or Arawak tribe?

As philosophers like Charles Mills have discussed, the abstract ideal of Enlightenment personhood assumed a racial polity that was white and male. Even the abstract, moral egalitarianism of Kant, which emphasized rationality and self-determination as the foundational markers of personhood rested on a dichotomy, or a "dark ontology," as Mills calls it, characterized by the willful and naturalized exclusion of enslaved and colonized persons from a discourse of rights and personhood.[21]

Thus when it came to personhood and the raced subject in the social and political discourse of the eighteenth century and beyond, the criteria of self-knowledge and self-assertion were replaced with the criteria of acknowledgment and recognition. Social personhood, in the case of the raced and colonized body, was an ontology not of self-determination but of other-determination, legitimated only through the granting power of a class that had already turned many of these persons into property. The willful omission of the raced subject from Enlightenment definitions of equality and personhood served to justify and perpetuate slavery, colonialism, and segregation well into the twentieth century and beyond.[22]

In nineteenth-century legal discourse, too, enslaved persons, while counted as "natural" persons, were also demarcated according to their condition as property and "sometimes ranked not with persons but with things."[23] Like Locke's anecdote of the prince and the cobbler, there was a difference in legal discourse between one's natural status as human and one's social status as person. Any man was a human, but only a man of social rank could be a person.[24]

But on both sides of the Atlantic and throughout the Americas, Afro-diasporic writers and activists fought back against this Enlightenment erasure through their participation in the public sphere. From the penning of slave narratives to the petition of freedom suits and land rights suits, these diasporic and native persons challenged their exclusion from the social polity by using the very technologies of print and public circulation of information that had marked, counted, legislated, hunted, and displaced their bodies (whether in slave ledgers, bills of sale, wills, land treaties, or fugitive advertisements) to instead now record and pronounce their socially recognizable, legally viable personhood.[25]

However, as scholars Jeannine DeLombard and Edlie Wong remind us in their important contributions to the role of print culture and legal discourse in the nineteenth-century construction of a diasporic "counterpublic," the act of making a claim for personhood or freedom carried inherent risks and contradictions, especially for the enslaved. Slave plaintiffs "assumed the guise of free persons to bring petitions for freedom even as the outcome of the trial was to determine their status." This "elliptical temporality" led to a performance of personhood that was always "belated and contingent" and that held within its very performance the potential of its negation.[26]

But in a strange yet predictable twist, it was often the charge of criminality *against* the slave that fully "activated his personhood," as

DeLombard explains: "Having been transformed from human property into legal person," the accused becomes a legible presence in the public sphere "through published trial transcripts, press accounts, scaffold orations, gallows broadsides, or pamphlet confessions."[27] Though it marked a punitive entry into political membership, the criminal justice arm of the law nevertheless had a socially transformative if ironic power, resuscitating the civilly dead human into the socially viable person. However fleeting and spectral this resurrection, it nevertheless laid the groundwork for alternative paths to African American civic presence, its constant circulation through newspapers and narrative inspiring activists like Frederick Douglass to learn to "talk 'lawyer like' about law" and to "seek *reentry* into the polity on more equitable, civil terms."[28]

Scientific narrative, I contend, played a similar role in this era, as a means of allowing a new, visible point of entry into social personhood, in part, as a result of its own accessibility and circulation, and in part, because of its emphasis on observation, experience, and encounter. When Darwin's *Journal of Researches* hit bookshelves in 1839, it was an immediate, global best seller. Science, even as it increasingly emphasized professionalization, specialization, and objectivity as its main aims, remained a discipline that was not one.[29] For it offered as much in the way of philosophy, literature, travel narrative, cultural study, and social theory as it did in the way of "pure" science. In fact, the term "science" did not become metonymous with "natural and physical science" until the middle of the century.[30] Not only did the wide circulation of scientific narrative, even during these professionalizing years (from popular science magazines and travel narratives to atlases and ethnological field studies) produce readers who could learn to talk "scientist like" about the new science, but the range of its journeys and encounters with others also provided a new avenue for the viability and legibility of diasporic persons, sometimes against its very intent.

Like the vexed role of criminal personhood, initial stagings of diasporic and indigenous personhood caught or marked by science did not by any means translate into heroic or redemptive acts of social inclusion. These displays (like photographic documentation, for example) were typically manipulated by scientists, readers, and viewers to further hierarchize, exoticize, and disenfranchise those whose voices they purported to unsilence, and/or whose bodies they made visible, as in the case of Louis Agassiz's South Carolina slave daguerreotypes and photographs of "mixed types" in Brazil, which I discuss in chapter 2.

Darwin himself, of course, participated in this staging of personhood, as he returned often (in his writings) to his encounters with native and diasporic people as he struggled with questions of species difference throughout his work, leading to several misappropriations of his overall theory of organic continuity. Darwin defined personhood through conscience or "the moral sense" (the ability to express sympathy, which is greater, even, than love), something that separated animals from persons. However, he remained conflicted by the differences he saw in behavior between "higher animals," like dogs and monkeys, and the "lower men" he had met throughout his travels, as he so deemed the Australians and the unacculturated Fuegians. Yet despite the fact that he would rather see himself as descended from "that heroic little monkey, who braved his dreaded enemy in order to save the life of his keeper . . .—as from a savage who delights to torture his enemies," Darwin had to admit that these were behavioral differences, *not* fixed biological—or even fixed cultural—traits. He experienced the relativity of these differences from the outset of his journey, of course, traveling with his fully acculturated Fuegian shipmates, who displayed as much moral sense when offering sympathy to the perpetually seasick Darwin aboard the *Beagle* as they did when comforting FitzRoy that they were doing quite well back home again. Personhood, in Darwin's scientific theory, as well as in his vexed social encounters, was a designation free of biologically determined gradations between humans.[31]

Such accounts, conflicted as they are, work to expand the archive of debates about personhood in this period and beyond. Scientific travel, as an always-already creolized project that merged a study of the diversifying natural and cultural spaces of the New World with the strict social order of the metropole, reflected and responded to these debates through its journeys and encounters in the Atlantic world. The artifacts and narratives of these scientific encounters with indigenous and diasporic persons represented and contributed to the reality of a world of cultures and peoples in flux. As I will show in the chapters that follow—through the transatlantic encounters of Charles Darwin; through the experiences of William James in Brazil and Pauline Hopkins's fictional Reuel Briggs in Ethiopia; and through the twentieth-century ethnographic performances of Zora Neale Hurston and Claude McKay in Jamaica, and of Katherine Dunham and Langston Hughes in Haiti—Atlantic persons continually participated in the construction of a scientific "counterpublic" that dislodged personhood from an Enlightenment definition rooted in teleological concepts of origin and self-continuity, emphasizing instead the dynamic process of change common to both biological and cultural life. This transatlantic personhood, as a status rooted in (or rather, routed through) movement, reflected far more accurately (and inflected with more political possibility) the performative, both/and dynamism inherent in Locke's example of the prince and the cobbler, of the "retractable personhood" of slaves in legal and literary discourse, and the ceaseless becoming and unbecoming at the heart of evolutionary theory.[32]

Undisciplined follows, as it progresses, the work of those raced subjects who stepped out from behind the lens of observation to become transatlantic observers themselves, performing the inherent interdisciplinarity and codependence of scientific and cultural inquiry. For even as scientific practitioners emphasized specialization and discrete boundaries for their work, scientific practice and its results had always drawn on multiple, overlapping fields and were unbound from any overdetermined narrative of singularity.[33] From the desire to build a static program of documentation and order, then, emerged a mobile and mobilizing language of the other, as observed subjects in the post-Darwin era slowly began to professionalize and move into the role of observers, effectively manipulating the performative nature of scientific inquiry by wresting the tools and strategies of observation and analysis away from their captors. In doing so, disciplinary border crossers like Hopkins, Hurston, McKay, C. L. R. James, Dunham, and Hughes also reveal the ways in which race is not simply a "fictional" category in the development of human societies but, far more crucially, a central factor in the formation, struggle, and dismantling of disciplinary thought.

Performance is critical to my raced interrogation of persons and disciplines in this era, as it is to all studies of race and diaspora.[34] But it takes on a particular resonance for a project concerned with ethno-scientific discussions of raced personhood, as a primary definition of "person" is itself rooted in performance. The *Oxford English Dictionary* defines "person," first, as "a role or character assumed in real life, or in a play, etc.; a part, function, or office; a persona; a semblance or guise. Hence: any of the characters in a play or story."[35] Such a definition brings to light the malleability, contingency, and, of course, the co-optability of personhood.

While performance theory in the past has been criticized for its links with anthropological projects tied to the perpetuation of imperialism, "in which the raw materials of the world (including its cultures and peoples) were and are grist for the colonial mill of western industry and capitalist production," theorists like Ric Knowles and others have introduced "a new kind of rhizomatic (multiple, non-hierarchical, horizontal) inter-cultural performance-from-below," which makes it an important part of my own methodological apparatus.[36] The "embodied practice" of perfor-mance offers a very particular way of knowing and seeing that emphasizes movement, presence, and exchange, mediating, as it does in my own work, between the "collective memory" of history, and the "new, potential, and virtual."[37] We see this, for example, in the work of Katherine Dunham, who brings together the diasporic histories of Haitian and U.S. culture in both her ethnography and her dance choreography, or in the dramatic representations of the Haitian revolution staged by Langston Hughes and C. L. R. James. This performative personhood is not always a celebratory position, nor does it always translate into legal and social legibility or rep-aration, but neither does it ask for permission or risk negation—it simply is and does. Confirmed by science and performed throughout the Atlan-tic world, this diasporic personhood brought increased attention to the hypocrisies of enslavement and colonization.

The Creolized Atlantic

Before the 1800s, the British Atlantic was a much more disciplining space, especially for the human commodities shipped across its waters. "Unlike the ship, which plied back and forth," explains historian Stephanie Small-wood, "the human commodities followed a relentlessly linear course: the direction of their transatlantic movement never reversed. Ships traced circles. Commodities traveled in a straight line."[38] But, in part because the New World African diaspora had been "nourished . . . by the peren-nial flow of captives on the slave ship's one-way route of terror,"[39] there was a gradual shift in subsequent generations of captives who stood on the shoreline of their now-native New World and watched new tides of ships come back in the historic wake of their parents' journeys. For them, the act of looking was not a backward glance to captivity but a forward vision that could promise escape and freedom. Also, as the African trade route became less populated by midcentury, more of these ships traveled within and across colonial coastal waters, transporting captives back and forth between colonial territories. These ships and the ocean upon which they traveled—once charting a singular course to captivity—now became more malleable spaces, fraught not simply with fear but opportunity. The Atlantic itself, then, was an undisciplining space that could, through the sheer act of movement across its waters, allow a status shift in the legal and social constitution of one's body.

In acts of shipboard rebellions, the ship, much like the ocean itself, transformed from a holding cell to a prosthetic extension of the fugitive slave's body—a vehicle of mobility and possible reconstitution—demanding recognition in its deliberate provocation of international conflict. In the case of the *Creole* (1841), U.S. slave rebels took over a ship en route from Virginia to New Orleans and demanded to be taken to a free Caribbean island. Although the rebels were taken into British custody when they arrived in Nassau, they were released weeks later. The other 116 slaves aboard were granted immediate freedom. It seems "The 19" rebels, and their leader, Madison Washington, were well aware that, under the Slavery Abolition Act of 1833, the British recognized African captives as colonial *subjects*, even if they had been deemed property under another nation's jurisdiction. Britain's decision not to extradite these men to the United States, as Maggie Sale details in her history of both the *Creole* and *Amistad* (1839) rebellions, "asserted a definitive position on an institution whose status was both changing and ambiguous."[40]

The rebels tested the legal enforcement of Britain's Slavery Abolition Act on international waters and also exposed the adaptability of a diasporic personhood whose "retractability" could work in a politically radical way. Donning British subjectivity as a strategic assertion of resistance to commodification, the rebels on the *Creole* illustrate the ways in which Atlantic spaces invited more complicated performances of personhood that mirrored, the (albeit, much more gradual) chaos of evolutionary performance—not always a progressive, teleological journey to freedom or liberation, but always a space of continual change, movement, and reconstitution.

While the fate of the freed Africans in Nassau has been lost from the historic record, their intra-Atlantic journey reminds us of the importance of the New World itself in the shaping of nineteenth-century science and personhood. Just as the Atlantic became an increasingly contested space in the nineteenth century, so the Americas had long been a space of cultural reconstitution—a space where kinship ties were constantly made anew and generations of creolized enslaved persons from across various parts of the Atlantic moved about and converged with new generations of voluntary and involuntary settlers alike. As anthropologists have noted, in regions where established creolized slave populations, as in the Carolina Lowcountry, were suddenly inundated with new Africans in the eighteenth century, "African culture was not surviving—it was arriving."[41] The space of the Americas continued to rehearse conflicting dramas of New World arrival for the repeated cycles of immigrants, settlers, and captives still crossing over and through its boundaries.[42]

Creolization, like personhood, is a term with a long and ironically territorial disciplinary history, in part because of its increasingly capacious geographic and intellectual terrain. Contemporary scholars have correctly criticized this very gesture of American societies and diaspora scholars to "recast creolization as a more fortunate process productive of cultures and individual abilities distinct from, and possibly superior to, those found in the Old World."[43] Creolization has had various overlapping and oppositional meanings for Caribbean and Atlantic world scholars, for postcolonialists, for anthropologists, and for literary theorists. From its rich history in the nineteenth-century Atlantic world as a term that articulated the fusion of European and African languages and persons in Caribbean spaces, creolization soon came to stand for the pan-African solidarity that shaped the Négritude movement of the 1930s.[44]

By the mid-twentieth century, historians and anthropologists Edward Kamau Brathwaite, Sidney Mintz, and Richard Price worked to extend this term to include and recover the traces of indigenous people wiped out by European contact and to embrace the presence of those outside the Afro-European diaspora who also contributed to Caribbean créolité, such as Asians and Middle Easterners. As Martinican writers Jean Barnabé, Patrick Chamoiseau, and Raphaël Confiant wrote in their 1989 declaration *In Praise of Creoleness*, "Neither Europeans, nor Africans, nor Asians, we proclaim ourselves Creoles."[45]

Later, postcolonial Caribbean scholars like Édouard Glissant and Antonio Benítez-Rojo insisted on a broader, yet unintentionally limited definition of creolization as an infinite and ceaseless process that does away with the notion of "fixed being" as a concept imposed by the West. In Glissant's formulation, colonial travel first instantiated the need to "fix" the notions of the rooted identity in the metropole. Conquerors became "the moving, transient root of their people," and the West is "where this movement becomes fixed and nations declare themselves in preparation for their repercussions in the world."[46] This confluence of colonial travelers, their (human) cargo, and the legacies of devastation, prosperity, or restructuring they wrought on those other continental points of the triangular trade carried the very contradiction to the fixed and rooted identity it so staunchly asserted. The desire to extend European personhood abroad led to its very disavowal in diaspora. Emerging from a European desire to expand, know, and fix the world into discrete and legible categories, the mission of colonial enterprise instead witnessed and contributed to this infinite process of creolization. But what such postcolonial readings often leave out is the role of interculture *already* at work in these sites, long before and well after European contact, and just as importantly, the continued significance of bounded local histories and identities in these spaces that cannot and should not be wiped out or dismissed in the wake of narratives of incessant change that are dangerously teetering on a tacit, if unintentional, acceptance of the neoimperial force of globalization—one that is already wreaking an all-too-reminiscent havoc on local communities. Such a reading—one that uproots notions of fixity and belonging from the Old World only to replant them in the New World—also risks denying the coevality of contemporary Africans, Indians, Asians, and indigenous groups across the globe.[47]

Thus, as contemporary historians and anthropologists have rightfully protested, creolization, as a term with such a complex and sometimes oppositional cultural history, has often been diluted of its specificity to simply stand as a synonym for cultural mixture, or worse, as a teleological narrative that is tinged with Herskovitzian celebrations of African continuities in the New World (a problem I take up, historiographically, in chapter 3). But the process of creolization—of disciplines and persons—is neither a teleological movement nor some fixed product of cultural fusion. Rather, it is a pattern of dynamic and ceaseless change, or perhaps, as Charles Stewart has suggested, a pattern of "restructuring." Stewart's more cautious formulation is attentive to the historical baggage of the term and moves us away from utopian and unidirectional understandings of it. "Restructuring can involve mixture," Stewart grants, but "it can also occur through the internal reorganization of elements or through a simplification of features without the addition of any exogenous elements." Creolization, in this sense, as I also read it, is the always-already there and elsewhere of intellectual and organic matter.[48]

The period under examination offers a moment in which this process was first articulated systematically in and as scientific practice, and eventually given a name: evolution. This scientific theory helps us to move away from an Enlightenment model of personhood rooted in a static and singular concept of self-continuity. It encourages, instead, the embrace of a diasporic model of personhood routed in the migration, multiplicity, and shifting relations and boundaries across cultures and territories alike.

Undisciplining the Nineteenth Century

The nineteenth century has historically been figured as *the* disciplinary moment in the modern history of the West, when the cataloguing and classifying of the natural world, and the regulatory structures of institutions and the state, imposed order and manufactured uniformity, offering a narrative teleology—perhaps even a kind of cultural caesura—to rapid societal and demographic changes. The nineteenth century was a pivotal moment in the instantiation of the catalogue and the state, as theorists and anthropologists like Michel Foucault and James C. Scott have outlined, and in the discursive transformation of "living beings" into "life" itself; a moment when events became the constitutive markings of History, and when historical documents, from passbooks to birth certificates, became the markings of legibility and state control—"the authoritative tune to which most of the population must dance."[49]

In *Discipline and Punish* (1975), Foucault points specifically to the nineteenth-century penal system, and the slow extension of its "penitentiary technique" onto the entire social body, spreading outward like a "carceral archipelago" from prisons to charitable societies to workers' lodgings, until "this great carceral network reaches all the disciplinary mechanisms that function throughout society."[50] This "calculated management of life," as Scott, Foucault, and others have traced, was a necessary function of power and order, a symptomatic reaction to the uncontainable proliferation of bodies and ideas. The emergence, then, of both biopower and modern statecraft was not a natural consequence of scientific or social change but an imposed project of colonization and control, glossed, as Scott reminds us, "as a 'civilizing mission.'"[51]

FitzRoy's own Fuegian "civilizing mission," coincident with Darwin's last-minute appointment to the journey, thus provides a fitting example, on a single ship, of the contrasting impulses to capture, discipline, and make legible, as FitzRoy wished to do with his Fuegian shipmates, and the impulse to absorb and experience the movement, change, and disorder of the organic world, as Darwin did on that same journey.

It is important to note, of course, that such a juxtaposition is not meant to assign a heroic or positivist role to any of the scientists and writers I engage in my work. While I do believe that evolutionary science challenged disciplinary logic by providing profound insight into the processual, networked, and disordered nature of living systems, this book does not privilege a phenomenological or subject-oriented approach. Like

Foucault, I believe that "the historical analysis of scientific discourse should . . . be subject, not to a theory of the knowing subject, but rather to a theory of discursive practice."[52]

Elizabeth Grosz, whose work also parallels this new era of science with shifting understandings of cultural and social life, explains the ways in which Darwinian science "transformed the concept of life, in quite dramatic but commonly unrecognized ways, from a static quality into a dynamic process." Darwin's writings offered a new expression of ontology for the nineteenth century and beyond, one in which "being is transformed into becoming, essence into existence," and "life is now understood, perhaps for the first time in the sciences, as fundamental becoming, becoming in every detail." Evolutionary thought thus also offers a new way of thinking about historical movement as unpredictable becoming, as "related species in the past prefigure and provide the raw material for present and future species but in no way contain or limit them."[53]

Unlike the ordered History that Foucault discusses and that has become synonymous with Enlightenment personhood and nineteenth-century concerns with classification, surveillance, and fixity, the historical movement to which Grosz alludes, and that I take up in my analysis, mirrors the "excessive productivity" of the evolutionary process, "with each culture an expression of its excessive and multiple possibilities of transformation and elaboration, each culture a surprise to and a development of nature itself."[54] Evolutionary process is not synonymous with the "natural history" that is the product of discourse and taxonomy as posited by Foucault, nor can it be tied (incorrectly, as it often is) to the imperialist rhetoric of racial superiority. Rather, this movement—dynamic, complex, shifting—is a reflection of both nature and culture in the modern era.[55]

"This dynamism of life," explains Grosz, "is not only cultural existence but also cultural resistance." Darwinian science, then, "provokes a concern with the possibilities of becoming, and becoming-other" which are vital to both biological and cultural life.[56] This dynamism was not a new process, but Darwin and other transatlantic travelers and writers offered, for the first time, a new articulation of this constant, dynamic movement of change, this ceaseless becoming and becoming-other. It is through such articulations and movements that we may begin to look at the Atlantic and the Americas as spaces that challenged the disciplining logic of the nineteenth century.

This disciplining logic works in two different but interrelated ways in my readings, as I am concerned with both the disciplining of persons (particularly through the legacy of enslavement, displacement, and racial classifications) and the concurrent rise of disciplinary fields like anthropology and biology from the mid-nineteenth century to the mid-twentieth century. Both of these concerns incorporate Foucault's dynamic understanding of "discipline" as both an act and a category that *contains* difference—carrying it as well as policing it. While this was, indeed, a period marked by the emergence of disciplines that sought to manage, name, and fix difference, they nevertheless reflected in their epistemic and literal boundaries a recognition of difference that threatened the static figure of the (white, male) human subject as the fiction upon which this disciplining logic was built, and the fiction that evolutionary theory actively unraveled.[57]

These disciplinary and regulatory forces were, indeed, forming, growing, legislating, cataloguing, and *fixing* others in their places. However, they were doing so as a symptomatic and anxious response to the proliferation of difference, a germ of resistance that could not, as the human sciences began to prove at this time, be contained or quelled. For "the real, geographic and terrestrial space" in which these disciplinary forces worked, as Foucault points out, "confronts us with creatures that are interwoven with one another, in an order which, in relation to the great network of *taxonomies*, is nothing more than chance, disorder, or turbulence."[58]

Yet discipline aims to neutralize even the effects of "counter-power" that may result from the imposition of order itself, from "the forces that are formed," as Foucault outlines in later work, "from the very constitution of an organized multiplicity," like slaves, for example (though Foucault doesn't specify), who may "form a resistance to the power that wishes to dominate it: agitations, revolts, spontaneous organizations, coalitions—anything that may establish horizontal conjunctions."[59]

The problem with this view of resistance is that it is still grounded in collective order, and privileges human desire—it is a horizontal conjunction, a human-centered, end-driven resistance. My focus, instead, is on the kind of ontology offered by Darwin's science, one that links his writings most directly with a non-subject-oriented humanities, and a processual but nonteleological vision of life, as Grosz once again also advocates in her most recent work.[60] This ontology is centered not on human life, but instead on "the relentless operations of difference, whose implications we are still unraveling."[61]

The aim of my own study is to prioritize these "operations of difference" over disciplinarity. For it is difference that compels disciplines and gives them their regulatory power, but it is also the key to their unraveling, as it is always moving and can never be contained. Although my analysis is necessarily human-centered, prioritizing racial difference and diasporic movement across the Atlantic as central to the destabilization of disciplines in the nineteenth and twentieth centuries, I am interested, like Grosz, in the broader "inhuman work" this difference can do.[62]

Thus my conception of personhood, though significantly and deliberately tied to the lived experience of persons, is meant to extend beyond human notions of subjectivity and disciplinarity. In this sense, it is like Darwinian conceptions of life itself as elaborated above; it is neither a fixed nor stable category of identity but can be understood only and always as a process of movement and mutability.

Personhood

As with disciplinarity, we may think of personhood as a term still entrenched in eighteenth-century European philosophies of self-knowledge and self-continuity, and the politics of legal fixity, surveillance, and control that came to define the century that followed. Scholars like Colin Dayan have referred to the legal acts of "making and unmaking persons" as a kind of "negative personhood," in which slaves, criminals, animals, and other detainees are "disabled by law." The meaning of "person" in legal terms, especially during this era, was "shifting and tentative" in similar ways to those I engage.[63] From freedom suits in the United States like those of Marguerite Scypion (1805) and Dred Scott (1857), to the Negro Seamen Acts (1824–26) and the second Fugitive Slave Act of 1850, personhood was a term bound directly to the regulation and disciplining of bodies in space. Yet the fraught, uncontainable nature of this term is precisely what necessitated its constant legislation, especially when its meaning could be challenged, and sometimes transformed, through acts of movement. Personhood could not function as a universal performative utterance, as "*I am*" did not hold up in a legal court for persons like Dred Scott and the 575 others who had sued for their freedom, in U.S. courts alone, by midcentury. Within the legal and classificatory discourse of the nineteenth century, one had to be interpellated and made legible by others as a person in order to be recognized and legally constituted as a person.

As a result, the human claims of identity, individualism, and embodied knowledge of the self had little bearing on a rights-based bestowal of social and political personhood.

I encourage, therefore, an alternate understanding of personhood, one that emerges not from legal or classificatory discourse but from evolutionary discourse. Just as Darwin himself struggled to map, in words, a process that could not be contained, and yet had to settle on *evolution*—a word that has been so misconstrued since then—so personhood becomes, for me, a similar rhetorical placeholder for a shifting, unbounded process whose very articulation in language fixes it in place, thereby contradicting what it does in practice. I track this parallel trajectory of personhood and science through an examination of encounter in the Americas—between European naturalists and indigenous, creolizing groups; between immigrant and African American artist-ethnographers from the United States and the native and diasporic peoples of the northern and southern Americas. By making encounter, not agents, the locus of political possibility in social, literary, and scientific discourse, *Undisciplined* interrogates the constructed ideologies of race and subjectivity in the modern West. By extracting the influence of science and scientific inquiry from a particular brand of European individualism steeped in fixed notions of race and progress, my interrogations reveal how a more open, transformative consideration of science and diasporic movement in this period can work to undermine not just disciplinary thought, but the very logic of slavery and imperialism itself.

I call on new materialist approaches that emphasize the importance of merging philosophy and history, natural and social science, to fully engage with an embodied but nonagential understanding of the material world. "Ontological commitments," as Stephen White has emphasized, are "entangled with questions of identity and history, with how we articulate the meaning of our lives, both individually and collectively."[64] But if we privilege articulation over function, we risk prioritizing a subject-oriented, positivist approach to science, which is precisely what my work seeks to overturn. Indebted to but departing from a Cartesian divide between matter and agency, new materialist philosophy insists instead on "describing active processes of materialization of which embodied humans are an integral part, rather than the monotonous repetitions of dead matter from which human subjects are apart."[65] In my own work, the static figure of the (white, male) human subject is the fiction upon which narratives of racial subjection are built, and the fiction that evolutionary theory actively unraveled.

But how might we begin to think about issues of nineteenth- and twentieth-century personhood and racial politics outside the realm of the subject? How can we engage what Denise Ferreira da Silva defines as an "analytics of raciality"—one that does not aim to transcend or obliterate racial difference, but prioritizes the productive centrality of race in the construction of globality—without fully attending to the constitution and function of personhood and subjectivity as fixed categories *within* the history of slavery and colonialism?[66]

To supplant a disciplinary understanding of personhood with a processual one enables a more radical politics of difference that moves beyond the management and ordering of it, the obliteration of it, or transcendence of it, all of which are by-products of a disciplinary order that privileges hierarchy and stasis. To undiscipline personhood is to recognize it not as the originary moment of *being*, but as a constant ontological process of becoming, which has powerful implications for a critical race theory that reimagines subjects, as theorists like Nikolas Rose, Gilles Deleuze, and Alexander Weheliye have articulated, as racial and technological assemblages, which have the ability to "change their properties as they expand their connections, that 'are' nothing more or less than the changing connections into which they are associated."[67]

The premodern era of the human sciences advanced boundaries between the human and the animal, the natural world and the social world that were "much more uncertain and fluctuating" than they became in the nineteenth century, after the formalization of the human sciences. The pre-Socratic Heraclitus, for example, also advocated a theory of *becoming* over *being*, postulating that "change is the fundamental reality rather than something derivative to be explained."[68] But by the nineteenth century, taxonomy had become the key to situating oneself amid the chaos of change, and self-recognition became the distinguishing feature of *man*— the exceptional animal who was human because he knew himself to be human.[69] Modern anthropology worked dangerously alongside this premise, functioning "by excluding as not (yet) human an already human being from itself, that is, by animalizing the human, by isolating the nonhuman within the human."[70]

Biology and anthropology emerged and traveled in a parallel trajectory in this era, struggling to assert the premise of human exceptionality in spaces that refused to yield to such disciplining categories as the subject and the self. Even postmodern anthropology struggled to come to terms with these more fluid notions of personhood it encountered in the field.

As anthropologist Clifford Geertz has famously stated: "The Western conception of the person as a bounded, unique, more or less integrated motivational and cognitive universe, a dynamic center of awareness, emotion, judgment and action, organized into a distinctive whole and set contrastively against other such wholes and against a social and natural background is, however incorrigible it may seem to us, a rather peculiar idea within the context of the world's cultures."[71]

Yet from E. B. Tylor in 1871 to Rane Willerslev in 2007, anthropologists have long noticed that personhood was a variable concept in the cultures they studied: "Rather than being an inherent property of people and things," personhood was constituted in and through relationships, a "potentiality" of "being-in-the-world" that could be granted as freely to animals as to people, depending on the context.[72]

Thus if we look at how the practice of biology and anthropology work together, not by prioritizing the end result of classification, nomination, or cultural translation but by examining the actual events to which its practitioners are exposed—different cultural practices, rituals, forms, and different organic processes, all in flux, transforming and transformative—we gain insight into the way difference works, in these spaces. For "it is hard to impose a notion of progress, of superiority and inferiority," as Grosz notes, and as Darwin found aboard the *Beagle*, "when the only criterion of success is the ingenuity of adaptation, and the only necessary proof of adaptation is our current existence."[73]

Darwin's writings, often cited for their dangerous alliance—through acts of manipulative misinterpretation—with social programs that used them to back their racist claims, actually provided a much more fluid, intertwined vision of nature and culture. The Darwinian moment thus becomes a vital mirror, as I will argue, for what had already been happening in the Atlantic space for generations; for the transformative change articulated in his science is based, in part, on his cultural encounters with Fuegians, Africans, and others. This theory of a world in flux contributed to a growing and diverse transatlantic archive—anthropological, literary, and political—that may now provide contemporary literary theorists, historians of science, and anthropologists with a fresh angle of approach to old narratives of nineteenth- and twentieth-century science and anthropology. Troubling as these narratives remain, we may now look upon them *evolutionarily* (that is, *non*-teleologically), with a broader understanding of race and difference as networked, mobile, and ontologically foundational to the construction of modernity and globality.

The mimetic acts inspired by the evolution of the human sciences alongside the continued experiment of colonial encounter also implore us to examine more closely the space between representation and authenticity. More specifically, they ask us to consider how (or whether) we can transform these stories of narration and representation into the so-called truth of personhood and experience, or into an active politics of justice. This has been the struggle of all disciplines of representation, including anthropology, which has historically been criticized, as Michael Taussig diagnoses, for engaging in the "redemptive" work of "rescuing the 'voice' of the [Other] from the obscurity of pain and time. From the represented shall come that which overturns representation."[74]

Such acts of mimetic encounter often appear as moments of literal or symbolic mirroring throughout my own work (as in the paragraph just above), but they offer neither redemption nor rescue. Rather, they exemplify the presence of an ongoing dialectic of disorder and undisciplining *through* and *against* ordered observation. Some of these "mirror moments," jarringly, even if fleetingly, did force observers to face the colonial violence of their gaze in the moment of encounter, yet also enabled them to justify their redemptive presence. However, if we attend carefully to these porous borders between disciplines and persons, between observers and observed, across the development of the human sciences, we increasingly find that the power of the representational moment—the moment of the mutual glance in the studied encounter—lies in its imminent potential to take down the hierarchical scaffold upon which it so precariously teeters.

In myriad examples of such moments throughout this work, both observers and observed move promiscuously through the looking glass of observation, often exchanging places as well as (and sometimes through their) glances, exposing this "colonial mirror of production" as the funhouse mirror of performative conceit it has, in fact, always been.[75] Thus the function of mirroring throughout this text is a deeply political one, in which the act of representation is overturned not by a validating, voice-granting presence but through the persistent subversion of the assumed order, authority, and stability of the representational lens.

Unraveling Subjects: A Narrative Overview

Undisciplined brings together four diverse but representative journeys across the Atlantic that reveal personhood as a diasporic process that reflected and influenced changes in scientific practice. I begin my investigations with Charles Darwin's encounters and travels with the native tribes of Tierra del Fuego, which helped to launch his theory of the living world in constant flux. Of course, this was not a novel concept in the natural sciences by the time of Darwin's journey. Geologists like William Buckland and Charles Lyell, and naturalists like Alexander von Humboldt, Georg Forster, Georges-Louis LeClerc Buffon, Jean-Baptiste Lamarck, Thomas Huxley, and Darwin's famous contemporary, Alfred Russell Wallace, had been hinting at geological and biological continuities, for many years.[76] What was new about Darwin's moment, and the century that followed, is the influence such scientific theories would come to wield on modern political understandings and cultural performances of raced personhood. As I move through the century, I also move back and forth across the Atlantic, from Tierra del Fuego to London, from Brazil to Boston to Ethiopia, from Harlem to Jamaica, and from Chicago and Harlem back to Haiti. This movement brings Darwin's journey into relationship with the exploitative photographic experiments performed by naturalist Louis Agassiz in Brazil, artist-ethnographer Zora Neale Hurston in Jamaica, and Katherine Dunham in Haiti, among other important figures (like Franz Boas, Melville Herskovits, Claude McKay, C. L. R. James, and Langston Hughes).

Chapters 1 and 2 thus chart a transformative moment in the nineteenth and early twentieth centuries, in which scientific disciplines were in flux, emerging and merging with one another as they shifted from truth-to-nature forms of pure observation to an interest in objectivity, to an emphasis on psychic experience.[77] I trace these transitions through the effects of cross-cultural encounter between Euro-American scientists and local inhabitants, from Tierra del Fuego to Brazil to Ethiopia. I begin with a history of European encounter in Tierra del Fuego, and its influence on Darwin's re-vision of the human. From there, I move to Louis Agassiz's documentation of the differences between "pure" and "hybrid" human types in Brazil, and the counterinfluence this journey had on the eventual political and scientific life of his own traveling companion, a young William James. Agassiz's attempted documentation of alleged degeneration through race mixture, in the form of portrait-style photographs, was aimed at proving that interracial union led to dangerous mongrelization and eventual extinction. Instead, this photographic archive offered a stunning narrative of resilience, survival, and a resistant refusal of the pseudoscientific gaze. It also had a lasting influence on the professional life of William James, then a medical student of Agassiz at Harvard, who signed on to the Brazilian expedition as an incidental traveler and collector, much like Darwin had done thirty years prior. James's own experiences with illness and recovery on the journey, and his encounters with the people of Brazil, inspired a very different kind of hybridity than the kind Agassiz sought in vain to document: a professional hybridity that went on to influence the work of W. E. B. Du Bois—quite directly—in his theories of double consciousness. James went on to work at the disciplinary boundaries of the psychic and the scientific, joined by contemporaries like Martin Delany, and influencing the work of other race scholars, too, like Pauline Hopkins, who found in his explorations of dual consciousness and the transpersonal, the transformative potential to shift the race "problem" into a race solution. Hopkins's *Of One Blood* (1903) takes up the work and path of James most directly, as it follows the journey of a mixed-race medical student at Harvard, secretly passing as white, who eventually learns that he is heir to the throne of a hidden but thriving Ethiopian kingdom. Hopkins's protagonist, Reuel Briggs, is a kind of composite figure of Delany and James, a medical student with mesmeric powers, whose own journey of double consciousness, self-discovery, and "second sight" comes through an archaeological expedition across Atlantic waters. The competing narratives of raced personhood at play in this chapter—of an ethnological exploration that linked racial mixture with degeneration and extinction, and a literary-psychological exploration that instead prioritized interracial union as the key to a noble, global future that merges the best of America and Africa in a single body—reveal the central importance of race in scientific and literary narratives of this period, and even more specifically, how the suturing of literature and science during this period encouraged an undisciplined and otherwise unimaginable portrayal of personhood as transhistorical, transpersonal, and inherently diasporic.[78]

Chapters 3 and 4 explore twentieth-century ethnographic encounters, alliances, and mentoring relationships that alternatingly encouraged and discouraged the study and assertion of personhood as a practice that precedes and exceeds taxonomies of self and nation. The creole performances of rebels involved in the Jamaican Christmas Revolt of 1831 highlight the broader historical shifts in the definition and performance of culture in the foundational, if controversial, work of ethnographers like Franz Boas, Melville Herskovits, Claude McKay, and Zora Neale Hurston. This section investigates the position of culture as both a shifting practice and an object of scientific study. As anthropology charted its course for the new century, its practitioners struggled to capture authentic moments of cultural practice without giving in to a Eurocentric approach to observation and study (often willfully resisting such approaches mandated by mentors and patrons), employing instead the basic tenets of a relativistic approach that was accidentally inaugurated by a British naturalist (Darwin) and retranslated for their field by a New World immigrant (Boas). But culture, like personhood, proves too elusive for any kind of capture, as ethnographers like Hurston would learn in their encounters with American peoples.

The book concludes with a backward glance at the long nineteenth century through the rich and vexed history of Haiti, and its profound influence on the larger diasporic consciousness of the Atlantic world. From the 1791 slave revolt that led to its eventual nationhood, and the ensuing refusals and exploitations that led to its eventual occupation by the United States from 1915 to 1934, Haiti's nationalism is nourished on narratives of displacement and belonging, revolution and accommodation. Focusing attention on the efforts of U.S. African American artist-ethnographers like Katherine Dunham and Langston Hughes to study Haiti illuminates the centrality of ethnographic performance to a more diffuse and global understanding of diasporic political formation. Haiti's precarious balance between indigeneity and foreignness, and its continued lore as central or exceptional to the New World story, helps us reconsider the very concept of "nation" itself, moving from a rooted understanding to a routed, diffracted one that revises European narratives of national unity.

I invoke writers like Édouard Glissant, Michel-Rolph Trouillot, Antonio Benítez-Rojo, C. L. R. James, and J. Michael Dash to help frame this discussion, as they are the first to offer a vision of the Caribbean archipelago as an open-ended global network with neither boundaries nor a center; one that resists fixed narratives of nation, and whose lens removes the space between observer and participant. I employ this vision to reveal the continuous relationship between indigeneity and foreignness as both constitutive of nationhood and threatening to its utopian logic of unity. Moving from personhood to culture to nation, this book ends with a claim that even amid the problematic, celebratory primitivism of the Harlem Renaissance, and the equally problematic nostalgia for Africa as the unrealizable myth of origin instead of a vibrant, contemporary partner in the struggle, what these twentieth-century artist-ethnographers actually performed was a narrative of common descent/dissent, bound not by captivity and linearity but, rather, a diasporic multiplicity of New World cultures and races. The ethnographic and literary components of Darwin's proto-evolutionary observations carried within them the logic that challenged Enlightenment notions of subjectivity. This, I claim, was the unique, inaugural dilemma of a new scientific modernity: nineteenth-century science both proposed a new theorization of the discrete Western subject and also confirmed—through the performance of its ethnographic others—the theory of its epistemic demise.

For Darwin, as for others in my study, narrative production is central to the construction and assertion of a subjectivity that is *disproved* in the moment of encounter. It is through an interrogation of these transatlantic encounters that this project intervenes in the constructed ideologies of race and subjectivity. Through a closer analysis of this space, I show how the Othered presences that reclaimed Atlantic waters have come to hail and dismantle disciplinarity, often using the same epistemic models that inaugurated the discourse of Western subjectivity to dethrone it.

1

Reciprocity, Wonder, Consequence

Object Lessons in the Land of Fire

The discovery of primitiveness was an ambiguous invention of a
history incapable of facing its own double.

V. Y. Mudimbe, *The Invention of Africa*

On March 5, 1834, the crew of HMS *Beagle* returned to Tierra
del Fuego to visit their once-captive charge, Jemmy Button. After a three-
year "adventure" across the ocean and back, as captive traveler with the
Beagle, Jemmy had been dropped off near his home territory in Wulaia in
January 1833. Now, fifteen months later, the crew of the *Beagle* returned
to find their shipmate utterly transformed in condition and appearance:
Jemmy, who had been "so particular about his clothes" and overall personal appearance during his British sojourn, was now "wretchedly thin,"
and "naked, like his companions," except for "a bit of skin about his loins."
The crew was also astonished to hear members of Jemmy's family speaking to FitzRoy in "Jemmy's English."[1]

Everyone had been altered by this collision of cultures, one that would
eventually have grave consequences. But one custom that remained
unchanged between the Fuegians and the British was that of gift exchange.
When Jemmy returned to the *Beagle* later that day in 1834, he came bearing gifts—two fine otter skins—"that he had dressed and kept purposely"
to give to his two closest friends from the crew, Dr. Benjamin Bynoe, the
ship's surgeon, and Mr. James Bennett, the ship's coxswain. He also presented FitzRoy with "spear heads and arrows of his own making" and
showed his British peers the canoe he had built, leading to their assess-
ment that he was, indeed, "well established" here. Darwin's diary also
noted, with a handwritten strikethrough that reveals the slippage involved

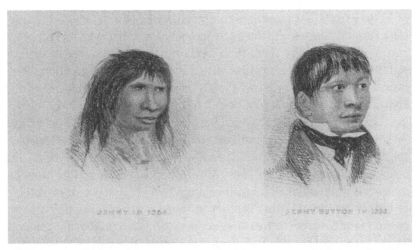

Figure 1.1. Jemmy Button in 1831, a year after his capture, and in 1834, after his time in England. From Robert FitzRoy, *Proceedings of the Second Expedition, 1831–36* (London, 1839). Reproduced with permission from John van Wyhe, ed., *The Complete Work of Charles Darwin Online* (2002–). (http://darwin-online.org. uk/)

in cross-cultural affiliation and colonial expectation, that the young Fuegian "had not the least wish to return to ~~his own country~~ England."[2]

Jemmy's hospitable gesture of welcome and reunion was actually part of a longer genealogy of reciprocity and exchange between Atlantic travelers and the local tribes of Tierra del Fuego. Often the first acts of engagement between many foreign travelers and local inhabitants, such exchanges became recurring cultural and narrative tropes in many European travel accounts. The ritual of gift exchange within these communities became the subject of Marcel Mauss's famous philosophical treatise on the cooperative nature of social relationships in so-called "primitive" societies.[3] For the Fuegians, as for many other American tribes, the outward spread of this exchange culture can be traced back to their very first encounter with Europeans, in October 1578. Sir Francis Drake and the crew of the *Golden Hind* "became the first outsiders to meet the southernmost inhabitants of the world." Drake and his men bartered with these Fuegians, most likely members of the Yamana and the Alakaluf, the southern and western tribes. As the ship's chaplain, Francis Fletcher, chronicled, "we had traffique for such things as they had, as chaines of certaine shells and such other trifles."[4]

These barters and exchanges continued, with Spanish and French travelers commenting on the Fuegians' exuberance over anything red—caps and combs and cloth—more than food or other items offered to them, a sign that confirmed their primitivity in the European imagination.[5] Redness, however, had obviously already made its cosmopolitan transition across the sea, waving back, as it did, from the hats and hands of Europeans. The familiar redness to which the Fuegians responded, as historicized by Michael Taussig in his brilliant study on the history of mimesis and the senses, is rooted in certain species of Indian and Brazilian trees. The color was discovered much later by European travelers, and its popularity spread throughout eighteenth-century Europe. But as redness fell out of fashion in the following century, it found itself crossing the Atlantic again, in the form of the treasured scarlet cloth so desired by the tribes of Tierra del Fuego. Redness had crossed the ocean, like Jemmy Button himself, and had come back home again. Thus these moments of gift exchange stand as powerful examples of the blurred distinctions between original and copy, foreign and familiar. The regifted red cloth made "a gift of what was in a sense a return, reissuing the exotic to the exotic from third to first, then First to Third world," rehearsing, as Jemmy's own kidnapping did, "the bewildering cross connections between gift, theft, and trade."[6]

By the time British sealer James Weddell encountered the Fuegians in 1823, just before Captain FitzRoy's first meeting, the Fuegians had grown accustomed to such exchanges. In November of that year, a few Yamana women in canoes greeted Weddell at St. Martin's Cove, just east of Hermite Island, near Cape Horn. Weddell, relieved that the women chose to remain in their own canoes, nevertheless made them a polite offering of "a little wine in a japanned cup." Once again, this "japanned" cup, as a European imitation of a Japanese style, complicated the First-Third world politics of reciprocity, origin, and mimesis. As anthropologist Anne Chapman narrates the encounter, "the wine spilt out while they were examining this marvelous container, which they 'cunningly retained.'" Not only did these women keep the object as the offering, but to his surprise and amusement, Weddell noticed the next day that, rather than making use of the container as a cup, the women had cut it into metal strips which they had then fashioned into necklaces.[7]

These exchanges, simple and brief as they are, have become part of the vast lore of Atlantic encounter and grow more significant with each retelling. As we learn from this last example between Weddell and the Yamana women, and as Darwin and others would later write, the Fuegian tribes believed in economy and equality in the division of goods. Whether a cup, a cloth, a whale, or the wreckage of a ship, the Fuegians shared equally with one another, taking great pains to divide everything fairly, as they did with the cup-turned-necklace. Stripped of its European cultural utility, the Japanese-inspired object now inspired a different culture in a new way.

As the years passed and the journeys continued, Europeans, U.S. sealers, and the native tribes of this region began to grow more accustomed, if not to each other's actual wants and needs, then at least to the lore of encounter passed down through journals and tales.[8] Nineteenth-century Atlantic travelers, for example, having read of the Fuegians' apparent fondness for this scarlet cloth, often waved it upon approach, or tied red tape to the foreheads of those they met, as an offering of peace. The Fuegians, having experienced the robbery of their furs and skins by these same travelers, often stripped off any garments before greeting strangers or boarding European ships.[9]

When FitzRoy and Darwin approached Tierra del Fuego from England with their three Anglicized Yamana charges—Jemmy, York, and Fuegia—in the winter of 1832–33, Jemmy is full of tales about how they will be greeted. As FitzRoy wrote in his *Narrative,* "the boy [Jemmy] was never tired of telling us how excellent his land was—how glad his friends would be to see him—and how well they would treat us in return for our kindness to him."[10] It is interesting that FitzRoy (in Jemmy's apparent words) has applied the notion of reciprocity to the act of kidnapping itself. The image of the Fuegians on the shoreline as grateful for the kindness shown to Jemmy is countered by the distress of Jemmy's mother. Darwin and the crew are told by York that "the mother had been inconsolable for the loss of Jemmy, and had searched everywhere for him, thinking that he might have been left [somewhere on the island] after having been taken in the boat."[11]

As European encroachment into the region increased, the system of bartering and gift exchange that had once made for relatively peaceful encounters grew more vexed and complicated. Anthropologists Marcel Mauss, Georges Bataille, and more recently, Michael Taussig have written about the role of gift-giving in societies in which collective accountability—a delicate balance between altruism and collective interest—supersedes the individual self-interest that is the guiding principle of European capitalism.[12] Though Mauss's anthropologically based treatise of collective responsibility stands as a marked response to the 1917

Figure 1.2. The Yamana greet the *Beagle* at the intersection of Beagle Channel and Murray Narrows. From Robert FitzRoy, *Proceedings of the Second Expedition, 1831–36* (London, 1839). Reproduced with permission from John van Wyhe, ed., *The Complete Work of Charles Darwin Online* (2002–). (http://darwin-online.org.uk/)

revolution in Russia, it is also relevant to these earlier examples of encounter between Europeans and Fuegians, which also reveal a mutual reliance on nonmarket principles of collaboration and exchange for Westerners as well as for the societies they encounter. Reciprocity and accountability become as necessary for peaceful Euro-American travel in this region as they are for the tribal communities themselves. As these groups grew more familiar with one another, their expectations and understandings of these transactions and their relationships with one another began to change. So, too, did their performance and understanding of personhood. While Mauss and others have traced genealogies, conceptions, and practices of personhood in both European and non-European societies, their studies rarely address the performance of personhood as a shifting consequence of cross-cultural encounter.[13]

For the Fuegians, such acts of gift exchange and reciprocity increasingly came to serve as willful assertions of equal personhood alongside the Europeans. In fact, the very name of the tribe that most frequently interacted with the Europeans, the Yahgan or the "Yamana," is also the word for "person," a simple but significant fact that brings to relief the importance of recognition in these cross-cultural interactions. For example, the constant "yammerschoonering" that plagues Darwin during his visit to Tierra del Fuego—the Yamanas' insistent phrase translated as a plea for goods and trinkets from their European guests—is also a word with a more complicated meaning than Darwin's rough translation of "Give me." Instead, as missionary Thomas Bridges later learns, the proper translation is, "Be kind to me." It is a phrase that not only demands recognition but also suggests indebtedness. For if the most recent round of European guests—sealers and explorers like Weddell and FitzRoy, among others—stole the Fuegians' food supply as well as some of their own *people*, it is only natural for them to expect something in return to balance this relationship: recognition, at the very least.[14]

Darwin, instead, tries to drown out this "yammerschoonering," ignoring every attempt at social recognition performed in the utterance of this complicated plea. Darwin had already intimated that he could imagine himself in the shoes of a slave before he could imagine himself a member of the Yamana tribe, a statement that reveals more about his discomfort with a rhetoric of cultural equality than an espousal of it.[15] The slave, and even the postemancipatory Afro-European, had a legible "place" within Western hierarchy that Darwin could safely and naïvely access as part of his social register. But these "savages," as socially unmoored from that European hierarchy, were too unstable and unbound from any legible cultural order that made sense to him, especially as their demands for equality and recognition grew more insistent. The Yamana Indians of Tierra del Fuego, by engaging with Darwin, and by refusing, with their very contemporaneous presence, his reading of them as spectral embodiments of his own ancestral past, continually reminded the young scientist of his *own* position of alterity on foreign soil, as an outsider in another group's home culture. Only his science could ground him in this unmoored space of human equality. Yet the wonder of nature's changeability also fed and confirmed his suspicions of a human cultural continuity that was constructed, adaptable, and ever-changing. Darwin's science proved a challenging retort to his own beliefs in social and cultural hierarchies of civilization and savagery, a hypocrisy with which he grappled throughout his life and his writings.

As evolutionary historians like Peter Bowler and others have discussed, Darwin realized from the start that the "new materialism" he proposed "had drastic implications for the status of man."[16] He was thus deeply invested in questions of psychological and social formation that would help him solve the riddle of how "man's supposedly unique characteristics could have been produced by natural evolution," and he read widely—from the work of fellow naturalists like Alexander von Humboldt and Robert Chambers, to political economists like Adam Smith and Thomas Malthus—in search of answers that might overlap. Bringing his own observations to bear on these earlier studies of geographic and social formation, Darwin reached his conclusion "that human nature is not fixed, but has been produced by a natural extension of the powers already possessed by animals."[17] Through his careful studies of geographic distribution in his 1859 *On the Origin of Species*—from geographic barriers that limited species movement to the environmental adaptations of those that did—Darwin showed that "the present relationships between living forms could only be understood as the result of a historical process."[18] He hypothesized further that "the greater development of human intelligence was the result of our ancestors adopting an upright posture, which freed their hands for tool making," thereby "accidentally providing an additional stimulus to the use of intelligence."[19] Yet, as Bowler explains, Darwin remained somewhat troubled by his own findings and assertions, and the coevality it seemed to imply between so-called "savage" and "civilized" men. Despite his revolutionarily modern suggestion, then, that "our mental powers are the result of a unique transition to bipedalism," and not "the acquisition of a large brain," Darwin moved quickly from biological fact to cultural construction, or from accident to intention, in his discussion of mental development, falling back on "the progressionist model" advocated by anthropologists and archaeologists of his day by presenting "the enhancement of our mental powers as though it were an inevitable consequence of natural selection."[20] For "as natural selection works solely by and for the good of each being," concludes Darwin at the end of *Origin*, "all corporeal and mental endowments will tend to progress toward perfection." There is, indeed, "grandeur in this view of life," he boasts.[21] But in waxing poetic about this incidental exaltation as a seemingly intended goal of evolutionary process, Darwin's language continually betrays his cultural desire for a linear progression that his scientific findings actively resist.

Yet even a cursory examination of the progression of Darwin's writing, from the personal narrative style of his 1839 *Journal of Researches* to the ordered prose of his 1871 *Descent of Man*, reveals an understandably dramatic shift—the maturation of a scholar who has honed his theory, the development of a writer who has honed his craft, and perhaps most strikingly, the change in observational style from the wondrous anticipation and capacious inhalation of an ardent field naturalist to the focused gaze of a laboratory scientist. By 1871, Darwin had learned to channel his foremost scientific tool—perception—from a panoramic exploration of the entire natural world to a concentrated, singular, yet connected object of study: the human. Though Darwin's primary interests in his early research years were geology and zoology, the foundational influence of the *Beagle* journey on his burgeoning theories of the human is not to be discounted. In fact, it was Darwin's few but important anthropological and ethnographic observations, especially of the native inhabitants of Tierra del Fuego, that left the most indelible impression on the young naturalist, and to which he would anxiously return in the years that followed.

Haunted by the commonalities he knew lay beneath the thin gauze of cultural difference that separated him from these men, Darwin tried to think through his anxiety, writing in an 1839 notebook, "your arguments are good . . . but look at the immense difference between man [and animals]—forget the use of language & judge only by what you *see*. Compare the Fuegian & Ourang outang & dare to say difference so great."[22]

Darwin concentrated primarily on the tools of observation here, but he also struggled to move away from a truth-in-nature perspective in order to take a more objective stance. Objectivity, as Lorraine Daston has historicized, became the hallmark of nineteenth-century science and required "the suppression of some aspect of the self, the countering of subjectivity." As immersed in the wonders of the natural world as he was, Darwin's "expansive mind" also required discipline and self-mastery. Ironically, it is through this disciplining of the self that Darwin could allow himself to imagine the undisciplined nature of human continuity across space and time.[23]

These recurring themes of perception and the place of the human in the scale of geological time came together for Darwin *first* in an anthropological context aboard the HMS *Beagle* in the 1830s and in his few but significant encounters with the Yamana, Haush, and Alakaluf tribes in and near Tierra del Fuego, where he puzzled over the seemingly single-generation shift between his three Anglicized traveling companions and their so-called "savage" brethren who greeted the ship on the wild and inhospitable shores of their native homeland.[24] Truth-in-nature could no longer be his guiding principle in a space where what he observed on land countered what he observed on board. As Darwin began to parse through these observations and beyond simply what he could *see*, he began the work of writing culture and science in a new way.

While scholars readily acknowledge the significance of Darwin's work for a number of interdisciplinary fields, from archaeology to biological anthropology, his influence on ethnography has not been considered as closely, even though the history and methodology of these ways of looking are so conjoined. Anthropologist Jonathan Marks cautions against the facile and metaphorical reading of a "Darwinian anthropology" that is rooted in Mendelian genetics, in theories of progress, in the genetic tracking of behavioral memes, in the linking of human and animal natures, or in the rejection of spirituality. I am not interested in any such generalized interpretations that risk propping up science as a simple metaphor for progress or cultural change. Instead, I am interested in historicizing Darwin's particular engagement with the world, and how his encounters, along with those that followed, worked to change scientific and cultural understandings and practices of personhood. These changes were, I believe, infinite and ongoing but not necessarily progressive nor in every case an adaptation. For it is true, as Marks states, that "along with the fittest, the merely fit survive." Evolution, indeed, is more "like a tinkerer" than "an engineer," as Darwin's scientific contributions would reveal.[25]

To historicize Darwin's position within the larger field of anthropology is to think, first, about his own position as a British writer and traveler whose literariness and imperial position creates a particular cultural narrative in itself, as both Mary Louise Pratt and James Clifford might attest.[26] Secondly, it invites us to look more closely at his treatment of the human *within culture* in these early musings, both on and off the *Beagle*, and how these lessons of cultural performance, cultural continuities, and cultural refusals shape his subsequent theories of the human, and the future of ethnographic thought. As a foundational discourse in replacing narratives of fixed identity with narratives of process and gradual change, evolutionary theory—a realization of the constitutional interdisciplinarity of the "life sciences" of biology and anthropology—catalyzed new conceptions of culture, race, and personhood with which the coming century would grapple.

Of course, Darwin was not the first to study, remark upon, and theorize the meanings of such continuities in his era. He joined a long trajectory of scientific travelers and writers who shaped his ideas, and who fed his curiosity, intellect, and wandering spirit, from the eighteenth century's most prolific natural scientist, Georges-Louis Leclerc de Buffon, to Buffon's most famous student, Jean-Baptiste Lamarck, whose contributions to a prototypical evolutionary theory Darwin would come to hone. Darwin's own grandfather, Erasmus Darwin, had also posited early evolutionary models in his 1794 *Zoonomia*.[27] The year of Erasmus Darwin's death, 1802, saw the publication of both Lamarck's *Hydrogeology* (providing the "first systematic account of the history of natural phenomena") and William Paley's *Natural Theology* (interpreting "the adaptation of each organic structure to its function as a sign of divine benevolence").[28] Robert Chambers's 1844 *Vestiges of Creation*, emerging (like Wallace's more provocative and scoop-worthy 1858 essay, "On the Tendency of Varieties to Depart Indefinitely from the Original Type") on the heels of Darwin's own work, discussed species transmutation but "adopted a very simple interpretation of the divine plan that was supposed to govern the process."[29]

But the foremost and most beloved scientist and explorer of this era, and the one Darwin would swiftly yet shockingly eclipse in recognition and notoriety as the nineteenth century drew to a close, was Alexander von Humboldt. Shocking, indeed, because Humboldt was—as scholars like Laura Dassow Walls and Aaron Sachs remind us in their beautiful recuperations of his work and influence—"the predominant intellectual of his age, the most famous scientist in the world, and, as was widely repeated, the most famous human being after Napoleon—a pairing that Humboldt, a loyal partisan of the French Revolution, despised."[30] Born in 1769 Berlin, and dying just six months prior to the publication of Darwin's *Origin*, Humboldt's influence on natural science, and on the transatlantic intellectual and cultural life of the late eighteenth through mid-nineteenth century, cannot be overstated. Humboldt, as Walls has described, was "the catalyst for modern science," adding, in the words of German physiologist Emil Du Bois–Reymond: "Every scientist is a descendant of Humboldt. We are all his family."[31]

In the New World and in the United States, especially, Humboldt was dubbed "the *second* Columbus," the "scientific discoverer of America."[32] In the continuous overlap of scientific influence, Humboldt himself was born the same year that Louis Antoine de Bougainville returned from his own circumnavigation of the globe, publishing his *Voyage Round the World* in 1771. Humboldt voraciously read Bougainville's account as a boy, as well as naturalist George Forster's 1777 account bearing the same name, of his own accompaniment, with his father, on James Cook's second voyage to the Pacific.[33] In finally meeting Forster through his faculty connections in 1789, explains Laura Dassow Walls, "it was almost as though Humboldt had met his older self." As Humboldt later memorialized him in his 1845–62 *Cosmos*, Forster ignited "a new era of scientific voyages, the aim of which was to arrive at a knowledge of the comparative history and geography of different countries," emphasizing not just details about specimens and navigation, but "the relations of climate and of articles of food in their influence on the civilization of mankind. . . . All that can give truth, individuality, and distinctiveness to the delineation of exotic nature is united in his works."[34]

Humboldt's own narrative through the Americas, published in 1819–29 as his *Personal Narrative*, is often paralleled with Darwin's *Voyage* (and, in fact, accompanied the young Darwin on his travels, at least the first of the seven-volume English translation, if not all of it, a parting gift from his mentor, John Stevens Henslow), but as historians have often noted, "the study of nature that led Humboldt to unity and harmony took a darker turn in Darwin's depiction of the inexorable struggle for existence."[35] Thus Humboldt has often been relegated to the realm of an "old-fashioned" Romantic idealism—"a colorful explorer, a romantic adventurer . . . an inspiration to the Hudson River school of painters"—until recent excavations have emphasized that his vision of "cosmic connectedness" was not so naïvely optimistic nor traditional in the least, but included both depictions of and a profoundly political philosophy against the "scenes of strife and violence" to which he was also exposed in his travels through the New World.[36] In the common patterns and connections he found across the Americas, Humboldt also found repeated evidence, both in the landscape he traversed and in the faces he met, of "the crimes produced by the fanaticism and insatiable avarice of the first conquerors."[37] As Walls has described, Humboldt "sorrowed at the vacant look of the missionized Indians, and pointed to their unchristianized fellows not as heathens or 'savages,' a word he repeatedly rejects, but as 'independent' peoples with their own distinctive character, dignity, language, and contribution to the great human story."[38] In "an otherwise beautiful" Cuban valley, Humboldt also lamented that "these plains are watered with the sweat of the African slave! Rural life loses its appeal when it is inseparable from the misery of our species."[39]

For Humboldt, as for Darwin, the naturalist's immersion into the landscape and the communities one observed was paramount to understanding the continuities between people and the environment. The complications they found there were strikingly different for each. Humboldt's vision of unity was hardly naïve, but it was complicated by the hypocrisies he found between spaces and rhetorics of beauty, liberty and expansion, and the realities of damage, enslavement, and destruction. Darwin's vision, in comparison, seems more naïve, complicated instead by *his* old-fashioned social beliefs in exceptional types that his scientific theory would not support. Thus Humboldt's politics were shaped and unified, not conflicted, by an understanding of how history and circumstance merged with science in the formation, adaptation, and obliteration of human communities. The progress of nations, Humboldt believed, "is helped or hindered not by internal, biological limitations, but by external, or environmental, circumstances and accidents."[40] Therein, perhaps, resides the most profound difference between these two particular explorers, influenced by many of the same thinkers, landscapes, indigenous and enslaved peoples: As Walls has proposed, their primary difference lies in purpose, as "Darwin was proposing a scientific theory, Humboldt a humanistic world-view." Anthropology, as a field, then, would come to occupy that crucial—albeit manufactured—space between them.

The roots of modern anthropology are often historically situated *after* the 1859 death of Alexander von Humboldt, *after* the publication, six months later, of *The Origin of Species*, and *after* the end of the U.S. Civil War. The Anthropological Society of London, preaching racial ranking and the "anatomic deviation of the Negro," was founded in 1863, shortly after Lincoln delivered the Emancipation Proclamation. The infamous American School of Anthropology, driven by polygenists like Josiah Clark Nott, Samuel Morton, and Louis Agassiz, that had come together shortly after Nott's 1854 publication of *Types of Mankind*, grew even stronger in the wake of the *Origin*'s transatlantic crossing. Positioning itself in opposition to the rising tides of politics and science, early anthropology sought to monitor and keep so-called "inferior" races in their social and biological place.[41]

Even the powerful monogenist thinkers who eventually paved the way for modern-day anthropological thinking—like American anthropologist Lewis Morgan, whose pioneering work on kinship studies in the late 1850s was overshadowed by Darwin's similar findings, and his British counterpart Edward Tylor, who was considered the "father" of cultural anthropology after the publication of his seminal 1871 *Primitive Culture*—still espoused, even as part of their ideology of a single human family, the limiting notion of "the unity of nature, the fixity of its laws."[42] But an interesting turn in anthropology began to emerge more fully in the new century, in part, as I will argue, because of the philosophical and cultural shifts that Darwin's writing and theories introduced and provoked. As writers and anthropologists began to articulate a vision of humans as organically connected to one another and to the larger natural world, the discipline was gradually appropriated by those historically and politically left out of its original narrative hierarchy: The captive human subjects of scientific and ethnographic inquiry, bound, even still, by its strict taxonomies of physiognomy and social hierarchy, nonetheless began to use its language to historicize, authenticate, and reassert their own position along the arc of culture. Jewish Americans like Franz Boas and African Americans like Zora Neale Hurston, for example, articulated the narrative of common descent in cultural terms, applying Darwin's theory to a new century.[43]

Disciplinarily speaking, the emergent nineteenth-century field of biology—the merging of zoology, botany, and physiology—was very broadly synonymous with "culture" and "life science."[44] Such a definition, in which culture is both a set of behaviors and customs tied to a particular group, and simultaneously a scientific and political act of promoting growth, change, and national improvement, connects it to the era's particular political and ecological ideologies of nationalism and imperialism; ideologies that linked cultural and scientific progress, in significantly contradictory ways, to Manifest Destiny and the ongoing discourse of natural rights.

However, if we bring Darwin's scientific observations and findings about common descent to bear on this definition, then this cultural-scientific *act* of promoting growth becomes simultaneously more nuanced and more simple—it is no longer an act that is willed or engineered by man but occurs in nature. "Nature," as Elizabeth Grosz has asserted, "is open to any kind of culture, to any kind of 'artificiality,' for culture itself does not find pre-given biological resources, but makes them for its own needs, as does nature itself. Culture produces the nature it needs to justify itself, but nature is also that which resists by operating according to its own logic or procedures."[45] Culture, then, in a post-Darwinian sense, is not a blind act but has a direction and pattern that is nevertheless free of values of improvement and superiority. Such a definition of culture, unmoored from human narratives of agency, makes clear that Darwin's theories of kinship and evolution are directly oppositional to the eugenic logic that drove popular (mis)conceptions of culture as a man-made agent of science.

Although the British scientific community did not commission any professional anthropological collections until the 1840s, FitzRoy and the

Beagle did bring back human remains from their journey: "A solitary pickled corpse," as Janet Browne has written, was brought back "in a barrel from the first *Beagle* voyage" and "was dissected at the Royal College of Surgeons." Two Yamana skeletons were also brought to Paris for study in 1883. But as Anne Chapman has noted, none of these people had been killed for scientific purposes. They had died of sickness.[46] In addition to these various "specimens," dead and living, that made their scientific crossing through Atlantic waters, Darwin himself expressed keen interest in the migration and linguistic patterns of the populations he observed there, as well as in the value of human artifacts, especially in the zoological and geological clues they provided. Darwin used such patterns to infer tectonic movements, and eventually, to inform his theory of transmutation.[47] He also had a keen intuition for native customs and symbols, understanding, for example, the value of a sacred tree in the valley of the Rio Negro that serves both as a symbol or embodiment of the Indian deity Walleechu, and as a directional marker "in a dangerous passage."[48] Darwin also relied on the presence and significance of artifacts as clues for deducing species origin and migration patterns. For example, as historian Sandra Herbert explains, "knowing the association of horses and hunting with bolas and finding arrowheads on the Patagonian plains led him to the conclusion not only that the Patagonian Indians had not hunted with horses but also that 'the horse was not an original inhabitant' of the continent."[49]

One might readily contend, of course, that these somewhat inadvertent examples of early fieldwork cannot, in any serious way, mark Charles Darwin as a pioneering ethnographer of South American Indian tribes. It is clear that Darwin had no desire to trace the languages and customs of these people as an end in itself. However, I contend that the way Darwin looks at the *entire* natural world (inspired, as it was by Humboldt and Lyell, among others)—and eventually, the way he fixes his gaze upon the Fuegians—sets a field-shaping stage (both because of his unique perceptual involvement with his landscape, and the ramifications of the theory of human kinship unleashed by it) for a century of scientific and ethnographic observers who follow. In fact, the very format of his field notebook links him to the world of anthropological observation as keenly as it does to scientific recording.

As a collector and naturalist, Darwin wrote, almost as a reminder to himself, in his *Journal*, "Let the collector's motto be, 'Trust nothing to the memory;' for the memory becomes a fickle guardian when one interesting object is succeeded by another still more interesting."[50] But the *objects* in any visual "field" are not always specimens that can be held, drawn, and collected. The Fuegians, the landscape, his own frailty as well as his own cultural difference, all compete, for Darwin, with his desire for immediacy, precision, and objectivity. As Michael Taussig notes about anthropological fieldwork, the "field" is "actually a meeting place of worlds, an interzone consisting of fieldworker and field creating therein a collage or intertext."[51] In this sense, the anthropologist, or observer, cannot simply present a one-dimensional *picture* of a three-dimensional exchange, for this "interzone" or "intertext" is a space of interaction that resists the act of documentation. The very act of recording this experience is, necessarily, an act of revision, or re-creation, "a switchback," as Taussig calls it, "by which one reality is pictured in terms of the other." Neither, in fact, can accurately render *what happened*, but provides, rather, "a picture of that which pictures it."[52]

Darwin's notebooks thus stand as metonyms for his own struggle and wonder at the undisciplined nature of his theory, and its implications for the status of man. For the notebook, as Taussig explains, "lies at the outer reaches of language and order" with its "ungrammatical jottings," its "staccato burps and hiccups," and because "it represents the chance pole of a collection, rather than the design pole." While a conventional diary might be ordered more chronologically and regularly "by the wheel of time," the field notebook is ordered by chance observations, encounters, and musings. Spontaneity and accident—not progress and intent—mark its constitutive framework.[53]

Readers are introduced, from the earliest moments of Darwin's 1839 *Journal of Researches*, and through his subsequent works, to his alternatingly relativistic and imperial manner of looking at the natural world, as he takes them on a vivid and often fantastic narrative journey through the Southern Hemisphere. Critical discussions of Darwin's narrative form highlight the accessibility of his language, as evidenced through the element of address.[54] Darwin, the curious collector, is a "voiced presence" who leads readers to things that he has "individually seen, heard, smelt, touched, tasted."[55] His touristic language is constantly addressing readers as if they are standing alongside their guide, asking them to "look at the family of squirrels; here we have the finest gradation from animals with their tails only slightly flattened. . . . Now look at the Galeopithecus or flying lemur."[56] As readers comply with his narrative request, they simultaneously navigate two contrasting worlds: a biosphere in gradual but constant flux, and a narrative bound and fixed by discursive limits.

Darwin does his best to overcome this narrative dilemma, employing a style that both interrupts and makes more accessible the temporal structure of his burgeoning theory. His language of address places readers in the present moment, while the abstract concept of his theory continually shifts them back to earlier biohistorical stages of species development, or propels them forward to imagine species extinction or modification through variation. Questions of origin, mortality, and survival through adaptability are couched within a presentist discourse that helps reorient readers from a linear model of deep time that would be impossible to envision or illustrate, into one in which the past is mapped onto the present and performed as such through narrative detail.

Darwin's early prose is full of sensual detail, from his imaginative description of gradual coastline formation through geological disturbances like volcanoes and earthquakes to the common habits, sights, and smells produced by marine animals, to the taste of sap produced by Chilean palm trees.[57] Darwin's journey is also colored by a large cast of human characters, from the maroon communities of Rio de Janeiro, the interesting and pleasant Gauchos of Montevideo, to the well-Christianized Tahitians, who are perhaps the favored of all the different indigenous groups he meets along his journey. Though some of his descriptions are only passing comments about dress or manner, the lasting impression for Darwin is always one of temporal instability. The Tahitians, "with their naked, tattooed bodies, their heads ornamented with flowers, and seen in the dark shade of these groves, *would have* formed a fine picture of man, inhabiting some *primeval land*."[58] These contemporaneous figures, set in a landscape (and an expressive medium—the field notebook) that is already unbound from historical fixity (the narrative moving from the present moment through deep time in a single sentence), function often as clues about the past. Darwin also understands his own liminal role, even if playfully at first, as one who is both observing *and* observed. Remarking on his own appearance before heading off for a day of field research, he writes, "with my pistols in my belt & geological hammer in my hand, shall I not look like a grand barbarian?"[59]

One might argue that Darwin's observational style during these early years was thus more firmly rooted in the curiosity of vision, rather than in the scientific mastery of a catalogue. In fact, his position throughout his research was often that of one whose involvement with the natural world required an un-knowing, a relinquishing of control in order to foster a deeper understanding of his kinship with it. His developing and oft-conflicting energies "to merge and to classify" worked best when he allowed himself to be prone. Like a specimen of the natural world himself, Darwin surrendered his body, placing it, as Gillian Beer has argued, "in a variety of relations to the physical world. Lying prone is both the naturalist's professional position for observation and, for Darwin, a pleasurable declension into the sensory world."[60]

As the curious student who immerses himself in the natural world in order to examine and imagine the common derivative history of all living organisms, often anthropomorphizing animals in order to vivify these commonalities for readers, one could argue that Darwin actually *performs* an evolutionary model of kinship with the natural world through language. Biographer Janet Browne consolidates some of Darwin's anthropomorphizing prose, especially during his time in Rio de Janeiro, where "flowers invited him to bury his head in their petals . . . and sometimes the rocks themselves were like people, hiding their secrets or teasing him with gnomic clues."[61] Through the language in his notebook, readers see his theory come to life, as the field notebook "becomes an extension of oneself, if not more self than oneself."[62]

In many of his descriptions, in an effort to retain some linguistic control, perhaps, Darwin often moves from the space of distant observation to the most intimate space of *ingestion*. He will often begin with the surface appearance of an animal or plant, move to the contents of its stomach or interior, possibly its appearance when cooked, and finally, to its taste. For example, the land lizards from the central islands of the Archipelago are described as "ugly animals" with "a singularly stupid appearance. . . . The colour of their belly, front legs, and head is a dirty yellowish-orange. . . . In their movements they are lazy and half torpid." After tracing the eating habits of these unfortunate reptiles, Darwin states that he has "opened the stomachs of several, and found them full of vegetable fibres, and leaves of different trees." After a detailed description of such contents, he goes on to state that "the meat of these animals when cooked is white, and by those whose stomachs rise above all prejudices, it is relished as very good food."[63] He goes through a similar litany with the small rodent, the agouti, of the Rio Negro, first describing its appearance, eating and reproductive habits, and finally concluding that "the flesh, when cooked, is very white; it is, however, rather tasteless and dry."[64]

Darwin's experiences often tend to move in this way, from observation to mastery, creating a narrative world that moves from a space of unknowing to one in which everything is knowable. Darwin plays the role of the omniscient narrator, even as his theory works against such a narrative of control and design. Even so, Darwin's rhetorical style, like his theory, is in a constant state of flux, sometimes playfully immersing the author in the fluidity of an ever-changing landscape, and sometimes anxiously asserting his control, pulling readers back into a discourse that is accessible but focused. It is through this rhetorical disorientation, explains critic James Krasner, that readers truly *experience* Darwin's theoretical development. "By involving the reader in a perceptual chaos that parallels . . . organic chaos," argues Krasner, "Darwin demonstrates the formlessness of evolutionary nature and the artificiality of a theory of distinct species."[65] Of course, this perceptual and organic chaos is not *entirely* synonymous with disorder. There is, indeed, an order and a pattern to the evolutionary shifts of the natural world, but this order is always shifting, adapting, building, changing—and it is impervious to the agency and willed order of man and language.

Darwin's struggle to articulate this chaos through the limited scope of language itself performs important cultural work: In attempting to *capture* his burgeoning theories about nature, species, and temporal continuities in language, Darwin, in fact, engages readers in what the Caribbeanist scholar Antonio Benítez-Rojo has referred to as the "sociocultural fluidity" of New World archipelagos like the Caribbean islands (or in Darwin's case, Tierra del Fuego). His revelations about scientific chaos are inspired by and paralleled with the "historiographic turbulence" and "ethnological and linguistic clamor" of the peoples he encounters in the Americas.[66]

As Michel-Rolph Trouillot similarly discussed in his writings about the Caribbean, "when E. B. Tylor published the first general anthropology textbook . . . in 1881, Barbados had been 'British' for two and a half centuries, Cuba had been 'Spanish' for almost four, and Haiti had been an independent state for three generations. . . . These were hardly places to look for primitives."[67] Despite the failure of missionary settlement in Tierra del Fuego, and their refusal to assimilate into a culture they found alien, Fuegian encounters with the West were also hardly novel by the 1830s. Thus the assertion of "primitivity," whether in postcolonial or uncolonized spaces, reflects a Western imposition of order and "tradition" that, as Trouillot emphatically noted, "succeeded modernity."[68] In other words, nineteenth-century Western traditions did not modernize so-called primitive societies, but, rather, these traditions imposed narratives of primitivism onto modern societies.

Darwin's pen, then, performs the instability of this Western imposition of racial order, as it works incisively to both *write* and *erase*, in this case, the boundaries between Europeans and their Fuegian counterparts. The imposition of order—the building block of imperialism and slavery—is, of course, dependent on language: history, temporality, humanity are all interpellated, ordered, disciplined by and through language. The impossibility of situating or translating the Fuegians in any coherent racial order—as immigrants, slaves, or colonial subjects—reveals for Darwin that social and biological taxonomies are linked in very similar ways: they are contingent, always shifting, never stable. His three different kinds of encounter with the Fuegian people—first with the Anglicized captives aboard the *Beagle*, next with the Yamana tribes they met along the shorelines, and finally, with the "re-nativized" Jemmy Button—revealed for Darwin that the social and biological are linked in unexpectedly fluid ways: as contingent, shifting, and never stable. Thus the claims of common descent and biological kinship made by Darwin the studied naturalist emerged from and mirrored the important perceptions and social interactions of an earlier, younger Darwin, the accidental anthropologist.

While the precision of his language is in part what makes Darwin's narrative style so compelling, its temporal instability sometimes leads to a loss of order and coherence at certain moments, especially when he is confronted with the seemingly anachronistic presence of the indigenous groups he encounters in his research travels. This linguistic (and perceptual) dilemma—the contradiction between the abstract concept of his burgeoning theory and the material expression of it—seems most clearly exemplified in his encounters with the inhabitants of Tierra del Fuego, whose contemporaneous presence yet "barbarous" ways create a desire for stasis in his narrative.

Although Darwin had already been traveling with Fuegians on the *Beagle*, he is not introduced to the local tribes "at home" in this region until the *Beagle* anchors in Good Success Bay, along the main southeastern shores of Tierra del Fuego, in December 1832. In the distance, the crew can see Selk'nam hunters standing on a cliff, and the next day, they meet members of the Haush tribe on land. Darwin writes in his diary that "while entering, we were saluted in a manner becoming the inhabitants of this savage land." From this salute, his description grows more fantastic and novelistic: "A group of Fuegians, partly concealed by the entangled forest, were perched on a wild point overhanging the sea, and as we passed by, they sprang up, and waving their tattered cloaks sent forth a loud and sonorous shout." These Selk'nam "foot people" follow the ship for some time, and then, "just before dark, we saw their fire, and again heard their wild cry."[69]

Immediately following his vivid description of the Fuegians' greeting, Darwin describes the natural landscape, stating that "the harbour consists of a fine piece of water half surrounded by low rounded mountains of clay-slate, which are covered to the water's edge by one dense gloomy forest." Just like his glance at the local inhabitants, "a single glance at the landscape" was also sufficient to show Darwin "how widely different it was from any thing I had ever beheld."[70] As Browne confirms, Darwin is "thrilled to the barbaric glamour of it all, the 'surrounding savage magnificence' of the country matching what he felt to be the raw brutishness of the inhabitants, feeling at last that he was on a real voyage of discovery, sailing to the uttermost ends of the earth."[71]

As in many of his other entries, Darwin wants to show that "the theatre" of the landscape is "worthy of the scenes acted on it."[72] In fact, in describing his first encounter with members of the Haush tribe on that December day in 1832, Darwin writes that this party of Fuegian men "closely resembled the devils which come on the stage in such plays as Der Freischütz."[73] His reference to Carl Weber's famous 1821 German opera not only showcases Darwin's desire for distance, by likening the lived experience of these contemporary persons to a theatrical performance staged for his awed amusement, but also ties the "legendary" status of the mythical "Freischütz" with the equally legendary status of the actual Fuegians. The six magic bullets of the "Freischütz," or "freeshooters," which never missed their mark, thanks to a Satanic contract, were the stuff of Germanic and Slavic folk legends from the fourteenth century onward.[74] Thus the Fuegians and the Freischütz share a common lore, in that their stories had been passed down as part of the European narrative tradition for centuries, but in Darwin's comparison, the Fuegians are relegated, once more, to the drama of historical fiction, not the reality of European conquest. Darwin's devils were not, in fact, the Fuegians, but the Europeans who came to make a deal. In the case of the three Fuegian captives, Jemmy, Fuegia, and York, the deal (that is, the successful "conversion" of Fuegian tribes) turned sour as soon as these captives were allowed back home again.

Scholars and travelers have given detailed accounts of the capture, return, and subsequent encounters with these three individuals, especially Jemmy Button. But the biographies of these travelers are limited by and to encounter. The stories of Jemmy and his traveling companions are filtered and available only through the lens of European colonial interaction. The *Beagle*'s Fuegian travelers were picked up during the ship's initial journey, in retaliation for the theft of one of FitzRoy's whaleboats. The first of these "hostages" was a "merry, happy" eight-year-old girl, a member of the Yamana tribe, who was given the name of Fuegia Basket, in honor of a wicker "basket" canoe that was built on Desolation Island by FitzRoy's men as makeshift transportation back to the *Beagle* after the whaleboat theft.[75] Fuegia's real name, prior to her kidnapping, remains yet a mystery. Though she later came to be known among her own people as Yorkicushlu, this likely intimated her adult status as "wife of" eventual fellow captive York.[76]

The young Fuegia Basket became a favorite among the crew members with her cheery disposition, and she was dutifully protected by another captive Fuegian who would later become her husband. This second hostage, El'leparu, was a member of the Alakaluf tribe, but the *Beagle* picked him up in Yamana territory, in March 1830. El'leparu was in a canoe filled with other Fuegians, and FitzRoy, fearing they would all board the ship and steal from them, initially ordered his shipmate Wilson to shoot above their heads to scare them away. But he suddenly thought better of it, deciding, instead, to take advantage of this opportunity to secure another hostage. He thus "recruited" the youngest of the group, a moody and sullen twenty-four-year-old El'leparu, to come aboard. The young man readily accepted FitzRoy's "invitation" by climbing into a boat lowered for him. As he was taken near the York Minster promontory, El'leparu was given the name York Minster.[77]

The third captive, who unfortunately died of smallpox soon after arriving in England, was a young man whose real name remains a mystery. Ironically renamed Boat Memory, in honor of the stolen whaleboat, this young man now stands as a spectral figure—his name highlighting the memory of traumatic journey, disappearance, and bodily theft. The twenty-year-old "Boat Memory" is the only one of the captives who was actually described as being very frightened when pulled aboard, and who "put up a mighty struggle in the water before being dragged, beaten and exhausted, onto the boat."[78] Most likely camping with his family on Whittlebury Island, where he was abducted, Boat Memory had nothing to do with the theft of FitzRoy's whaleboat.[79]

In May 1830, the *Beagle* took its final and most famous captive, the young Jemmy Button, a teenager from the Yamana tribe. Jemmy and some family members approached FitzRoy and his men, who had been out in a small cutter, exploring the Beagle Channel area. Jemmy's people arrived in three canoes filled with fish and skins as offerings of peace, with the customary hope of reciprocal exchange. The Europeans had already bartered with local tribes on Navarino Island earlier that day before heading back out toward the Murray Narrows, where they encountered this new group of Yamana. In their earlier encounter on shore, they had bartered "beads and buttons for fish. Fitz-Roy exceptionally offered a knife for a very fine dog," which the natives were reluctant to trade, but eventually did.[80]

Now, in this later encounter at the intersection of the Beagle Channel and Murray Narrows, an even more reluctant (and likely unintended) transaction occurred, as FitzRoy invited a fourteen-year-old boy to board the cutter. In exchange, FitzRoy handed his uncle a mother-of-pearl button. This is how Jemmy "Button" received his new surname, despite the ambiguous nature of the trade that landed him his special place in the history of British encounters with the Yamana people. Jemmy's real name was eventually recorded as "Orendelicone." George Despard, an Anglican missionary who worked with Jemmy and his family from 1858 to 1860, was the first to discover this, though he writes also that the name, when translated to English, means "Unknown." This seems a fitting name (or more likely, a fitting misnomer) for a historical figure who remains profoundly unknowable to this day.[81] In this strange economy where the lines between gift and trade, hospitality and reciprocity, have always been blurry, it is unclear whether the Fuegians understood the meaning of this final transaction. Had they deliberately engaged in human trade, or were they simply allowing the child to have a brief, touristic adventure aboard the foreign boat?[82]

As FitzRoy's anger over the stolen whaleboat began to cool, he also came to the gradual realization that his young captives—from different tribes and different areas—could not be properly and safely landed in their home districts. FitzRoy had to make alternate plans. It is then that he transformed these captives, in his mind and in his narrative, into *charges*, and decided to bring them back to England. In so doing, he was also able to transform the narrative of his reckless act of kidnapping into a noble act of "deep responsibility." He would educate and Christianize his young charges—at his own personal expense—and bring them back to their homes on his next expedition, where they would serve as translators and help spread Christianity throughout their homeland.[83] So the Fuegians embarked on their own transatlantic journey, stepping onto British soil in the fall of 1830, studying at St. Mary's Infants School in Walthamstow, and eventually even meeting with King William IV and

Queen Adelaide before returning home aboard the *Beagle*. An eager but nervous young missionary, Richard Matthews, was chosen to accompany the Fuegians back to their homeland, despite FitzRoy's worries that "a single man cut adrift in a 'savage' landscape" would have a difficult time in the harsh environs of Tierra del Fuego. But in December 1831, the *Beagle* set sail once again, embarking on what would be a most memorable journey for FitzRoy, the three Fuegians, Richard Matthews, and a student named Charles Darwin who was chosen at the last minute to join the expedition.

Through his own curiously mimetic interactions with his newly assimilated Fuegian traveling companions, who were still learning about British language and customs, Darwin was also able to view himself, at various points throughout the journey, as a sort of specimen. He, too, was an object of curiosity for the Fuegian travelers, just as they were to him. For example, Jemmy was fascinated and perplexed by Darwin's persistent sea-sickness. "The notion," for Jemmy, "after his aquatic life, of a man being sea-sick, was too ludicrous, and he was generally obliged to turn on one side to hide a smile or laugh, and then he would repeat his 'Poor, poor fellow!'"[84] Darwin was also in the habit of comparing his natural abilities to theirs, noting that their eyesight and auditory capabilities were much stronger than his and that "they could make themselves heard at treble the distance of an Englishman."[85] This later helped Darwin to conclude that heightened sense perception was a necessary attribute for human survival in adverse conditions.[86]

The Fuegians were apparently conscious of their superiority in this regard, and at various times had "declared what some distant object has been, and though doubted by every one, they have proved right, when it has been examined through a telescope. They were quite conscious of this power; and Jemmy, when he had any little quarrel with the officer on watch, would say, "Me see ship, me no tell."[87] Thus the Fuegians' superiority extended beyond sense perception to communication, as they frequently engaged with and playfully teased their British peers aboard the ship. In fact, both Darwin and FitzRoy affirmed that the Fuegians showed a particular ease with language acquisition, especially Fuegia, who managed to pick up both Portuguese and Spanish while the *Beagle* was docked in Rio de Janeiro and Montevideo, along with English.[88] Once again, the Fuegians' sociability, and their ease with outsiders, could not be considered too novel in an era when encounters with others were so frequent.

Fuegians had always been described, even amid awful depictions of their "wretchedness," as resourceful and sociable.[89]

Although Darwin was continually impressed with the Fuegian travelers' basic command of English language, and their sometimes keen, sometimes playful interactions with their British shipmates, he was frustrated that he was unable to learn much from them about the habits of *their* fellow countrymen. In his questions and observations about their religious beliefs, for example, he was able to glean only that they had some "superstitious" notions, but that these were not much different from those of the other sailors on board. However, over time, Darwin was able to learn, through observation and conversation, that Fuegians "sometimes bury their dead in caves, and sometimes in the mountain forests"; he learned that "Jemmy Button would not eat land-birds, because 'eat dead men'"; and that "each family or tribe has a wizard or conjuring doctor, whose office we could never clearly ascertain."[90] He also learned that some of the Fuegian travelers' religious assertions—perhaps stated as reactions against the biblical teachings to which they were exposed in Britain—were tied to a sense of patriotism for their native land. Jemmy, for example, was full of praise for "his own tribe and country, in which he truly said there were 'plenty of trees,'" and criticism for other tribes, stoutly declaring "that there was no Devil in *his* land."[91]

Thus Darwin was well acquainted with Fuegians long before the *Beagle* ever reached their homeland. The contrast between his own shipmates and the Yamana people he met along the shoreline was therefore terribly exaggerated by his exposure to these three individuals. Through these encounters, Darwin begins to understand and articulate a concept of relativity that also accounts for gradation, difference, and change. The Fuegian "other" is not a relic of a past era, but a contemporaneous, transforming *presence*. The possibility of such a successful assimilation, and subsequent, alleged "reversion" revealed, for Darwin, the tenuous position of acculturation and allowed him to fix his attention more fully on the human. "Of all Darwin's varied experiences during the voyage," writes Janet Browne, "it was this recognition of the connections between humans around the world that moved him the most. . . . He was forced to acknowledge that the gauzy film of culture was nothing but an outer garment for humanity."[92]

Through his ethnographic encounters with Fuegians in varied modes of mimetic cultural performance, coupled with this new way of seeing the natural world, Darwin's theory begins to come into focus. "Nature," notes Darwin, as he explores the Fuegians' native habitat, "by making habit omnipotent, and its effects hereditary, has fitted the Fuegian to the climate and the productions of his country."[93] One might make the counterargument that, by attempting to turn the moment of spectacle into a pedagogical space about species and societal development, Darwin attempts to regain narrative control and distance himself from his Fuegian kin.

But this is where Darwin's scientific reliance on materiality and perception—the key components of his narrative architecture—help him (and his readers) resist the limits of language. As stated earlier, the concept of evolution, while aimed at decentering the preeminence of the human, is necessarily expressed through the disciplining language of human experience *and* Western hegemony. Darwin's language thus seems to create a seemingly inescapable dilemma for evolution, as it attempts to impose a "methodological control" (epitomized by the embodied address of the Western observer) onto a theory that has no place for it. However, Darwin's close encounters with other humans, along with his reliance on perceptual language and readerly address, do betray the manipulated fiction of language in two fundamental ways. First, the role of senses like *taste* and *sound* in this perceptually driven narrative represent the "space" where language can move *beyond* the methodological control of the narrator, connecting the bodies of readers with the bodies of those represented within the narrative world. Second, as essential components in the very nature of observation, the senses as observational tools are inherently tied to the mimetic dilemma of representation itself, as we have seen throughout the continued contact between Europeans and Fuegians. In these encounters, it is difficult to know just who is mirroring whom as the layers of cultural borrowing and interaction inform and build upon each retelling.[94]

Thus the very gesture of representing the Fuegians, from the sounds they make to the foods they eat, to the colors that move them (expressed in the same bold, sensual language Darwin uses to describe the rest of the natural world) performs kinship even as it appears to resist it. For Darwin, this additional mimetic relationship to nature itself ties his experience to the Fuegians (and to ours, as readers) in an intimate, familial way, again, both through and against the disciplining force of language.

It is through a more careful consideration of this earlier vision that we begin to understand the significance of its maturation from his discussion of natural selection in his 1859 *On the Origin of Species*, to his discussion of sexual selection and human evolution in his 1871 *The Descent of Man.* A cursory reading of the latter work, especially, may lead to a misunderstanding of it as a text that accepts the hierarchical differences between the various races of man. However, a closer examination of the language used by the mature Darwin reveals the lessons he has learned from those early years of wondrous observation. He understands the culturally imposed urgency to assert the differences between man and other animals, or between "civilized" and "barbarous" races. Yet he returns, at every opportunity, to his experience with the Fuegians as one of the most significant lessons in teaching him otherwise: "I was continually struck with surprise," he writes, "at how closely the three natives on board *HMS Beagle*, who had lived some years in England and could talk a little English, resembled us in disposition and in most of our mental faculties."[95] Even if one were to admit a "wider interval in mental power between one of the lowest fishes, as a lamprey or lancelet, and one of the higher apes, than between an ape and man," explains Darwin, one must also recognize that even this seemingly immense interval is "filled up by numberless gradations."[96]

While this later writing does account for a perceived difference in "moral disposition" between "a savage who does not use any abstract terms, and a Newton or Shakespeare," Darwin is quick to reiterate throughout the text that these differences are neither fundamental nor fixed. "Differences of this kind between the highest men of the highest races and the lowest savages," writes Darwin, "are connected by the finest gradations. Therefore it is possible that they might pass and be developed into each other."[97]

The subtlety of Darwin's phrasing in *The Descent* may also be misleading, especially in moments when he himself accounts for the difference between *language*—which is necessarily classificatory and static in its function (as that which designates and names)—and the evolutionary *process*, which defies such categorization. This is evident, for example, in his discussion of the scientific obsession to rank and separate the races of men as distinct species. "The most weighty of all the arguments *against* treating the races of man as distinct species," announces Darwin from the outset of this discussion, "is that they graduate into each other, independently in many cases, as far as we can judge, of their having intercrossed."[98]

He then goes on to list the numerous orderings by different scientists, in a somewhat tongue-in-cheek catalogue: "Man has been studied more carefully than any other organic being," writes Darwin, "and yet there is the greatest possible diversity among capable judges whether he should be classed as a single species or race, or as two (Virey), as three (Jacquinot), as four (Kant), five (Blumenbach), six (Buffon), seven (Hunter), eight (Agassiz), eleven (Pickering), fifteen (Bory St. Vincent), sixteen (Desmoulin), twenty-two (Morton), sixty (Crawfurd), or as sixty-three, according to Burke."[99]

Darwin uses the inconsistency of these rankings themselves to prove his point, paralleling the diversity of judges with the diversity of races themselves. He states such a "diversity of judgment," while it "does not prove that the races ought not to be *ranked* as species," nevertheless shows that "they graduate into each other, and that it is hardly possible to discover clear distinctive characters between them."[100] There seems to be something interestingly performative about the function and ordering of language itself here, as Darwin suggests that anxious naturalists might console themselves by *fixing* and ranking mankind, in some articulate order of classification, in as many different species groupings as they wish, but the fact remains that there is no actual *biological* ordering or locatable measure of species difference in the variations of mankind. Classification and order thus exist only in language, not in organic processes, which are constantly transforming, multiplying, and resisting the imposition of linguistic ranking. Darwin concludes this section by aligning himself with those who have tried, and failed, to find order and meaning in such rankings, stating that "every naturalist who has had the misfortune to undertake the description of a group of highly varying organisms, has encountered cases (I speak after experience) precisely like that of man; and if of a cautious disposition, he will end by uniting all the norms which graduate into each other as a single species; for he will say to himself that he has no right to give names to objects which he cannot define."[101]

The influence of Charles Lyell's *Principles of Geology* on Darwin's own preliminary theories is well known. But while Lyell's rhetorical method reflected, like his theory, a uniformitarian scale that never disturbed the reader's sense of equilibrium, Darwin's rapturous looking often reflects "a multiplicity of forms" that must be recognized together. This perceptual play forces readers, like Darwin himself, to "continually reorder" the visual field. But in the moment of anthropological pause, both Darwin and his readers rehearse a new way of looking that shapes his future work and vision. When Darwin finally fixes his gaze upon the Fuegian, he begins to "keep his eye stationary and envisions analogous forms in the same visual space." James Krasner refers to this shift in Darwin's observational style as "evolutionary vision."[102]

This evolutionary vision, recorded in language, is the key to understanding Darwin's anthropological influence. The study of humans—their rituals, languages, cultures, traditions, and intellectual capabilities—were vital to Darwin's evolving theory of adaptation and development, of the interplay between order and change. Darwin's fixed gaze, then, was neither about stasis nor about progress but, rather, about the continuity and mutability of existence. For Darwin believed, as Elizabeth Grosz has argued, in "the plurality, or perhaps even the relativity, of social, moral, and aesthetic categories. It is hard to impose a notion of progress, or of superiority and inferiority, when the only criterion of success is the ingenuity of adaptation and the only necessary proof of adaptation is current existence."[103]

In his 1871 *Primitive Culture*, anthropologist Edward Tylor points to the white man's hermeneutic failure in his relations with indigenous tribes, stating, "we can have no difficulty in understanding how savages may seem mere apes to the eyes of men who hunt them like wild beasts . . . who can only hear in their language a sort of irrational gurgling and barking, and who fail totally to appreciate the real culture which better acquaintance always shows among the rudest tribes of man."[104] Tylor sees this failure of interpretation as a sign of the *white man's* degeneracy, a loss of "real culture" and language on the part of the voiced observer. Darwin risks a similar misinterpretation as someone who does carry himself through his travels with an air of cultural superiority as an emissary of the British Empire and as an observer who struggles with the parallels between wild and domestic animals and savage and civilized men throughout his journey.

But once again, it is the "failure," from FitzRoy's perspective—of the Fuegian experiment that has a transformative, relativizing influence on Darwin and his theory of the human. After his first contact with Jemmy, York, and Fuegia, Darwin determined that their three years among British society had sufficed "in contradiction of what has often been stated . . . to change savages into . . . complete and voluntary Europeans."[105] In fact, he was so certain of their transformation that he feared they would no longer fit in their native homeland. Yet Jemmy's stunning renativization just a year later comes as a great shock to both Darwin and FitzRoy.[106] Once again, it is Darwin's ethnographic encounters that help to expand and hone his evolutionary vision, forcing him to concentrate more carefully at the "analogous forms" and shared, cross-cultural histories in his ever-expanding visual field.

Such vision, or more broadly, perception, represents both the loss of a certain fantasy of linguistic certainty for Darwin, as well as the space where language can move beyond the scientific or hierarchical methodology that attempts to shape and limit it, connecting, for example, the bodies of Fuegians with the bodies of all future readers in a gesture that begins to dismantle the "mediated colonial relationship" through the mimetic act.[107] Darwin's anthropology thus reveals how the process of cultural un-knowing—through sensory declension and a surrendering of linguistic control—can lead to a broader understanding of kinship, race, and the constructed space between the "primitive" and the "civilized" that grew to be a late-Victorian obsession.

Darwin's narration of his Fuegian encounters, in part, sets this stage, revealing the futility of imposing order, mastery, and supremacy on a theory whose foundational principles depend precisely on a lack of such mastery and supremacy. In *Descent*, Darwin insists "that man and the higher animals, especially the Primates, have some few instincts in common. All have the same senses, intuitions and sensations—similar passions, affection, and emotions, even the more complex ones; they feel wonder and curiosity; they possess the same faculties of imitation, attention, memory, imagination, and reason, though in very different degrees."[108] It is the burgeoning realization of these instinctual similarities, some forty years earlier, that evoked a most productive narrative anxiety in Darwin in his *Journal of Researches*, and that would continue to stoke the irrepressible cultural anxieties about racial and cultural proximity for a new generation of transatlantic scientists and anthropologists on the brink of a new century of encounter and performance.

The social consequences of scientific and imperial encounter demanded from Darwin, as for others, a more fluid engagement with (if not understanding of) personhood as an act of mutual constitution and negotiation between cultures. European personhood and Fuegian personhood, as this chapter has shown, are neither oppositional nor teleological positions but, rather, intertwined and reciprocal, dependent upon one another for survival and self-knowledge in unfamiliar spaces. In the years following Darwin and FitzRoy's final departure from Tierra del Fuego in 1834, Euro-Fuegian tensions surrounding issues of conversion and reciprocity began to mount. The latter half of the nineteenth century saw an increased missionary presence and the rise of colonial interests in the region. By the 1880s, Tierra del Fuego was divided up between Argentina and Chile, and native tribes began dying at a more rapid pace. But in the half century between Darwin's visit and this final colonizing drive of the 1880s, British missionaries like the Alfred Gardiners (father and son), the Reverend George Despard and his adopted son, Thomas Bridges, and ship captains like William Parker Snow and Robert Fell all maintained close ties with the local tribes. But as the years progressed, some of them, most notably and fatally, Captain Fell, often manipulated the Fuegians' cultural reliance on reciprocity and exchange, using bribery tactics to transport Fuegians back and forth from the missionary settlement on Keppel Island and making young men labor for food and other goods.

These European missionaries, in need of translation assistance and inspired by the tales of Jemmy Button based on the previous narratives of FitzRoy and Darwin, often took to calling any helpful Fuegian leader "Jemmy." British missionary Allen F. Gardiner met a man from the Selk'nam tribe he called "Jemmy" in December 1850, though this Jemmy was neither as polite nor as welcoming to strangers as the "real" Jemmy.[109] It wasn't until five years later, in November 1855, when Captain William Parker Snow miraculously hailed the actual Jemmy by shouting his name from the deck of the *Allen Gardiner* (named in honor of the missionary cited above, who succumbed to starvation, along with his crew, during the previous mission voyage), that the "real" Jemmy resurfaced. Snow writes of his interpellation of Jemmy in his journal:

> Then, to my amazement and joy almost rendering me speechless—an answer came from one of the four men in the canoe, "Yes, yes; Jam-mes Button, Jam-mes Button!" at the same time pointing to the second canoe . . . [to] a stout, wild, and shaggy-looking man standing up . . . "Jam-mes Button me! James Button me!", shouted the newcomer; "Jam-mes Button, me: where's the ladder?" And the next moment Jemmy Button—the very man himself—the protégé of Captain Fitzroy—the one upon whom the mission rests so much of its hopes—was alongside, well and hearty, and giving me a welcome in broken words of my own tongue! . . . The next instant he . . . was on the deck of the "Allen Gardiner," shaking hands as heartily and as friendly as if he had known us for years.[110]

It was Snow, with his warm demeanor and kindness to Jemmy, who convinced the young man to bring his family for a brief stint at Keppel Island.

But Jemmy's suspicions increased as he tired of his position as an object of study. At one point during their time together, Snow showed Jemmy the sketches FitzRoy had made of "his" Fuegians (see figure 1.3 below). Snow describes Jemmy's reaction to these mirrored portraits as alternatingly amused and sad, as he looks upon the sketches of his peers, as well as the dual character format in which he himself is depicted, as both "savage" and "civilized." "Which he thought [amused or sad], he did not choose to say," writes Snow, "but which I inferred he thought was gathered from his refusal to go anywhere again with us."[111]

Snow did not push Jemmy to return to the mission or to recruit other young men to join him there. As a result, Snow was fired by Reverend George Despard, the senior missionary, who arrived at Keppel Island and set up his own family there (including his two sons, Francis Jones and the thirteen-year-old Thomas Bridges, who would go on to become one of the most famous missionary workers in the region), leaving Snow and his wife stranded in Port Stanley for several months until they could find alternate funding and transportation home.[112]

Despard made a concerted effort to distinguish the work of missionaries from that of colonists, surveyors, and the "men of science," who he felt had squandered the trust of the local tribes, making their own work more difficult. "They are not well disposed to white men," he wrote of the Fuegians, "and for good reason, for the white man passing along their shores has subjected them to every kind of bad treatment: he has shot them down for amusement, saying 'come, let us have a shot at those niggers.' They have been killed by the men of science, who thought they had nothing better to do, than . . . to put them to death, for the sake of bringing their dead bodies over to Europe and dissecting them."[113] Of course, as scholars like Chapman and Browne have already documented, and as mentioned earlier, these men of science did not murder local people in cold blood for the sake of research. While it is true that many generations of Europeans were likely complicit in the illness or disease that killed even the few specimens of Yamana remains that were brought back to England and Paris, these were not people who had been murdered by scientists but, rather, bodies that were posthumously collected for scientific study.[114]

The only "successful" missionary interventions, fleeting though they were, had a similar aim as science in these years: Men like William Snow; the young Gardiner, who stepped in after him in 1857; and Thomas Bridges, who would follow in their footsteps, all sought to establish some

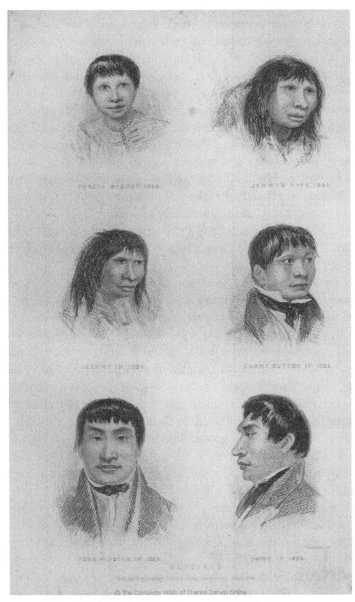

Figure 1.3. FitzRoy's Fuegians. From Robert FitzRoy, *Proceedings of the Second Expedition, 1831–36* (London, 1839). Reproduced with permission from John van Wyhe, ed., *The Complete Work of Charles Darwin Online* (2002–). (http://darwin-online.org.uk/)

sense of understanding and continuity with the local populations. Jemmy Button was, for as long as he lived, their crucial link.

The young Gardiner found Jemmy in much the same way as Snow did, simply by approaching four canoes in the distance and calling out "Jemmy Button" until someone stood up and answered, "Yes sir." After an exchange of gifts between the men, including a box of carpenter's tools sent to Jemmy by his old friend, Dr. Bynoe, Jemmy essentially led Gardiner and his crew on a tour through the history of his encounter with European missionaries and men of science, leading them to the spot where FitzRoy had built huts for the first missionary, Richard Matthews, who had accompanied the Fuegians back to their homeland in 1833.[115] By gaining his trust and listening to Jemmy's wish that families be allowed to travel together to Keppel, Jemmy agreed to ask for the consent of his tribe to take his own family to Keppel, where they might serve as an example for other families.

Jemmy and his family spent a pleasant five months at Keppel with the Despard family, though they were anxious to get back home, having agreed to come simply as a gesture of courtesy and public relations assistance for the settlement. No doubt they enjoyed their celebrity status, and enjoyed a special rapport with the Europeans. But once Captain Robert Fell got involved, transporting Jemmy and his family back to Wulaia territory in November 1858, the relations between these two groups began to turn more visibly sour. Jemmy noticed that the rules of reciprocity were no longer fairly or equally applied. At the mission, he and his family members were treated as proper guests. But upon their return back home, they were expected to work. Jemmy and his brothers "hauled trees," "stripped bark for the frame of the mission house," and "were paid a number of biscuits corresponding to the hours of work" they put in.[116] Jemmy registered this sudden shift in treatment and, of course, was unhappy about the increased labor he had to perform. He is said to have whispered to one of the other missionaries that "Captain Fell give other man clothes, no give my countrymen clothes?"[117] Jemmy also inquired one afternoon about his lack of breakfast, asking the captain in an irritated manner, "What do you call that, no biscuit, no nothing, to eat?"—to which Fell retorted back, taking on "pidgin" English for his reply: "No work—we no can give biscuit."

While Jemmy had long understood his position as a studied and coveted subject, he could not endure the affront of this blatantly hierarchical model of recognition and reciprocity. He now actively retreated from the spotlight, preferring to keep a lower profile, but advocating for family members who still wished to be involved with the mission. He dined with Despard for the last time aboard his yacht in late December 1858, during which time he told him that his brother, Billy Button, wished to join Despard and his wife at Keppel and that arrangements should be made. The Despards happily obliged.[118]

But the spotlight continued to follow this most famous figure of the local community. Ten months after his dinner with the Despards, in November 1859, the same month as the publication of Darwin's *Origin of Species*, Jemmy Button was implicated in a massacre of Europeans in Wulaia Bay. Eight members of the crew of the *Allen Gardiner*, including Captain Fell and his brother, were brutally murdered with stones and clubs while they gathered for Sunday services at the recently constructed mission house on shore. The day prior to the massacre, members of the crew noted that "about seventy canoes arrived and some three hundred natives had assembled," but no one registered this as a threatening arrival.[119] It is unclear whether this organized attack was a violent reaction of the local tribes to their ill treatment, forced conversion, and deteriorating relations with Europeans, or whether it was simply a territorial war between the Yamana and the Selk'nam, or both tribes unified against the Christians. The formal story is that a group of Selk'nam fighters, well known for their violent tendencies, descended upon the crew of the *Allen Gardiner* at about half past ten in the morning of Sunday, November 6, during a weekly church service at the mission, killing all but the cook, Alfred Cole, who had stayed behind on the ship to prepare the midday meal. Jemmy Button was in the mission house at the time of the murders—whether as witness or participant remains unanswered to this day.

Cole managed to escape after the attack and survived in the woods for several days with the help of local tribes in the area. In a surreal and macabre performance of their desire to divide their share of the wreckage equally among themselves, Cole recalled the sight of several Fuegians dressed in the clothing of the dead crew members, who gave him food and shelter in the days following the massacre (most likely members of the Yamana tribe and not the Selk'nam warriors who had been implicated in the murders—though it is unclear, due to the nature of the massacre, which group was, in fact, responsible: The Yamana had a long and fairly amicable history with Europeans and were also not known as warriors, like the Selk'nam, but as fishermen, or "canoe people." Yet Fell and his men were killed with stones and other rudimentary weapons, wielded more often by the Yamana people, than with the spears and more sophisticated weaponry typically used by the warrior Selk'nam clan). These Yamana also took all of Cole's clothes in exchange for the food they gave him, and left him "wearing" only a coat of paint. Cole saw "a man in a canoe" who "was wearing a sweater that had belonged to one of the men who had been killed and another had on Captain Fell's blue coat."[120] In Wulaia, Cole was reunited with Jemmy and his family, who brought him clothes, including the late captain's boots, and fed him. These Yamana people had donned the clothing of the fallen crew like some kind of spectral drag show, wearing the shirts and jackets of their British peers, many of them ripped and torn for the purposes of sharing with others from the community. And yet, as Cole recalled: "I lived with them pretty well on shellfish, fish and mussels. . . . Sometimes the men would go out at dawn and come back by sunrise, with a great load of fish &c. They treated me as one of themselves."[121]

Cole also testified that tribal members told him that Jemmy and some of the other Fuegians had returned to the ghostly *Allen Gardiner* on the night of the massacre and that Jemmy had slept in the captain's bed. Jemmy denied this in his own deposition, though the gesture could signify any number of emotions, from triumphant displacement to grief and mourning of one leader over the loss of another. Whatever the circumstances or exact facts of the massacre itself, it does seem that, in the days that followed, the Fuegians took on a different kind of self-possession. Denied equal treatment and reciprocity while Fell and his crew lorded over them, the Fuegians now took and divided everything of these men between themselves upon their death. Once again, we are caught in the mimetic process, that "intimate web of copy and contact," as local tribal members eagerly sought to equalize the relationship by taking on the costumes and roles of those who sought to "own," "steal," or convert them.

Jemmy was held in custody for two months at Port Stanley, questioned about his involvement in the Wulaia Bay Massacre, and eventually released. He testified that while he was, in fact, present at the start of the attack, he witnessed only the murders of Captain Fell and the ship's carpenter before the Selk'nam murderers demanded the departure of all local tribal people. Jemmy explained that he initially tried to protest the attack, but fearing for his own life and the well-being of his people, he chose to flee the scene as the Selk'nam demanded. He later returned to bury four of the bodies of the murdered English crew.[122] The official transcript of Jemmy's inquest, conducted by Governor Moore and the colonial chaplain, Captain Smyley, took place in the Colonial Secretary's Office of the

Falkland Islands on March 12, 1860. Jemmy's responses (often to questions that are missing from the transcript) indicate that the primary concern of the Colonial Office was not the murder itself but, rather, Jemmy's feelings about the Missionary Society and Europeans in general, and how the different tribes communicated with one another. Jemmy explains at the start of the deposition that he "staid at Keppel Island four moons with wife and children" but that he "Did not like to . . . don't want to; don't like it."[123] Although such questions about his feelings and his people (however they had originally been framed) were purportedly aimed at establishing motive and potential conspiracies, Jemmy's testimony also confirms and parrots what the British Colonial Office had suspected: that the missionary project was a failure and that the Fuegians were forced to go to Keppel against their will. The Patagonian Missionary Society feared that the Colonial Office would ultimately hold them accountable for their role in exacerbating tensions between Europeans and local tribes.[124] But in the end, it was neither the evangelical project nor its cultural consequences that would significantly reduce missionary work in the region but, rather, the rise of epidemic disease that would infiltrate the region—a direct biological consequence of encounter.

The long history of European experiment and investigation in this region—from the mapping and naming of trade routes, to the scientific observations about human migration, adaptation, and survival, to the social experiment of colonial settlement and Christian conversion—reached their culmination here, with the testimony of a man who understood these complicated relationships perhaps better than anyone else, coming of age, as he did, in their presence. Jemmy Button, from his first to his final encounter with his European charges, mirrored their journeys, their observations, their hopes, their skepticism, and their cross-cultural transformations. Through his years of cultural contact and cultural transference, Jemmy stands as the quintessential figure of cross-disciplinarity for this group, as one who had spent his life straddling dual and dueling worlds, First and Third, scientific and social, observed and observer, serving as linguistic and cultural translator for a generation of Europeans in Yamana/Selk'nam/Alakaluf/Haush territory, and for a multitribal Fuegian community on the verge of extinction. Jemmy Button, like Darwin himself, was a key performer in the reconfiguration of personhood in the nineteenth century from a discourse of static self-knowledge to a shifting act routed through centuries of increasingly complex modes of encounter, study, and exchange.

2

Of Blindness, Blood, and Second Sight

Transpersonal Journeys from Brazil to Ethiopia

The Peoples of the Sea proliferate incessantly while differentiating themselves from one another, traveling together toward the infinite.
Antonio Benítez-Rojo, *The Repeating Island*

As evolutionary ideas progressed from Darwin's encounters with indigenous peoples around the globe to the living rooms and lecture halls of Europe and the United States in the second half of the nineteenth century, they hastened the emergence as well as the dissolution of many strands of scientific and philosophical thought. William James was a young student at the recently established Lawrence Scientific School at Harvard University in Cambridge as Darwin's ideas crossed the ocean after the publication of *On the Origin of Species* in 1859. He had a prime seat, in September 1861, for debates that ensued between faculty members like Louis Agassiz and Asa Gray, who argued on opposite sides of the evolution question.[1]

The eldest son of a prominent theologian but an early proponent of Darwin's theory, James found himself both riveted and vexed by the scientific and social changes proposed by evolutionism, and he worked throughout his own long career at the interstices of scientific and religious thought.[2] From medicine and physiology to psychology and philosophy, from pragmatism to spiritualism, the professional trajectory of William James from 1861 to 1910 serves as a prolific example of the undisciplined, permeable, and overlapping nature of intellectual and scientific discourse in this period.

James prioritized experience over observation as a preferred mode of scientific and philosophical inquiry, eventually situating his ideas within the theory of pragmatism, a branch of American intellectual thought that traced its roots to these same young Harvard scholars whose ideas had percolated together on campus. This group, the Metaphysical Club, included James himself, along with logician and mathematician Charles Sanders Peirce, and lawyer and eventual Supreme Court justice Oliver Wendell Holmes Jr., among others. It represented only one of several philosophy clubs that had sprouted in this era, as scholars and thinkers tried to absorb the vast intellectual conflicts wrought by sweeping social and scientific changes. They met informally from 1871 to 1879, and it was here that early conversations about pragmatism first took place. However, the term was not formally introduced into public discourse until 1878, when Charles Peirce published a pair of articles collectively titled *Illustrations of the Logic of Science.*[3]

Pragmatism, in Peirce's definition (though he would later call it "pragmaticism" to separate his original formulation from others), is a consequentialist theory: the truth or validity of an object or concept is determined by its practical application or effects. An object is hard, heavy, or strong if it proves itself, in practice, to be so. Likewise, a concept is true if inquiry confirms it, albeit with an essential recognition of the potential fallibility and partiality of any truth claim. William James took these ideas a step further, offering pragmatism as a method of inquiry that might help intervene in seemingly "interminable" metaphysical disputes between science and religion. James looked to pragmatism as "a mediating philosophy" that could reconcile "the scientific loyalty of facts" with "the old confidence in human values and the resultant spontaneity, whether of the religious or of the romantic type."[4] My interest in James rests on the application of this romantic "spontaneity" of human values and behaviors to scientific and political thought. For it is through an examination of these often unquantifiable, untraceable excesses of the human—lineage, memory, consciousness—that we can begin to understand how science makes a space for the performance of a raced personhood that is both unclassifiable yet vital and visible.

In an 1898 lecture, "On a Certain Blindness in Human Beings," James cites a passage from Robert Louis Stevenson's essay "The Lantern-Bearers" (1888) to illustrate his own shared ideas about the limits of observation and narration, and the primacy of experience:[5]

The observer (poor soul, with his documents!) is all abroad. For to look at the man is but to court deception. We shall seek the trunk from which he draws his nourishment; but he himself is above and abroad in the green dome of foliage, hummed through by winds and nested in by nightingales. And the true realism were that of the poets, to climb after him like a squirrel, and catch some glimpse of the heaven in which he lives. And the true realism, always and everywhere, is that of the poets: to find out where joy resides, and give it a voice far beyond singing.[6]

The detached observer in Stevenson's example, like a scientist with his scribbled-in notebook, "his documents," cannot truly *see* "the man." These young lantern-bearers on the links might appear "to the eye of the observer," as "wet and cold and drearily surrounded; but ask themselves, and they are in the heaven of a recondite pleasure, the ground of which is an ill-smelling lantern."[7]

To "catch some glimpse of the heaven in which he lives," writes Stevenson, we must rely on the poets and writers to "climb after him" and give a voice to this experience.[8] James spends nearly the entire lecture ventriloquizing the work of writers and travelers, those who have experienced "other" worlds, from poets like William Wordsworth and Walt Whitman to naturalists and travelers like William Henry Hudson, who reveal to "us," the intellectual elites who idealize "indoor academic ways of life," our own blindness to worlds and lives and "forms of existence other than our own."[9] Through their writings and travels, we learn about the "savages and children of nature," writes James, "to whom we deem ourselves so much superior," but who "certainly are alive when we are often dead." The result of these considerations and quotations, he implores at the conclusion of his essay, is a command "to tolerate, respect, and indulge those whom we see harmlessly interested and happy in their own ways, however unintelligible these may be to us. Hands off: neither the whole of truth nor the whole of good is revealed to any single observer, although each observer gains a partial superiority of insight from the peculiar position in which he stands."[10] As an active member of the New England Anti-Imperialist League, James used this lecture, among others, to condemn U.S. intervention in the Philippines and elsewhere. In a later delivery at the Cambridge Conference in March 1899, for example, James adds a blunt moral to the end of this lecture, stating, "That this is not altogether without its bearing on our supposed national duty of instructing the Philippine Islanders in life's absolute values need hardly be pointed out."[11]

"On a Certain Blindness in Human Beings" is a lecture thus caught somewhere between burgeoning cultural relativist ideals and laissez-faire politics. James is hardly advocating the kind of tolerance and engagement that could be considered inclusive, humanitarian, or even fully cognizant of the increasing interdependence of global cultures and economies. His own anecdotes throughout the piece are also riddled with language that fetishizes and infantilizes the alleged simplicity of other cultures. The larger, yet more simplistic, blindness at work in this piece is one that the anti-imperialists and pragmatists might agree upon: the hypocritical blindness of a nation allegedly founded on the lofty ideals of freedom and self-government, now imposing its imperial will on global others. The nation's long-standing hypocrisies with regard to "freedom" and "empire" were neither novel nor surprising for its own domestic "others." But for at least a few members of the white elite of Cambridge, the hypocrisy, it seemed, had finally hit home.

James's rhetorical strategy is, nevertheless, to point this blindness outward, as a disease of passive spectatorship, not of willed erasure. In asking his audience to consider "the blindness with which we all are afflicted in regard to the feelings of creatures and people different from ourselves,"[12] James does not demand collective reckoning with the nation's historical and contemporary treatment of racial others at home (though he does share an anecdote about his own initial blindness to the simple but rich cultural life of mountain dwellers in North Carolina). Rather, by stringing together a series of artistic and cultural examples to illustrate how cultural blindness operates, James, in fact, invites his audience to take a more calculated, scientific look at the distance between ontology and spectatorship in general. Although his advocacy of a "hands-off" approach to respect and tolerance does nothing to remedy past wrongs or to encourage future alliances, his litany of examples that sutures scientific looking to artistic expression and everyday life opens the door to professionalizing long-standing questions about the study and experience of consciousness and raced personhood. These questions would take scientific center stage at the turn of the century and would have a profound impact on the scholarly and creative work of scientists, artists, and philosophers like James himself.

For James's theories about cultural blindness and the importance in understanding the profound gulf between "the subject judged" and "judging spectator" were literalized some thirty years prior to the penning of this lecture, when he found himself—as Darwin did thirty years prior to that—aboard the steamship *Colorado* as a young collector, accompanying his professor and mentor Louis Agassiz on his 1865 Thayer Expedition to Brazil and the Amazon. In a journey best and shamefully remembered for the clandestine photographic experiments conducted by Agassiz in a failed attempt to prove the degenerating effects of racial "hybridity," James's experience stands as an interesting counterexample of a burgeoning intellectual vision of cultural continuities, and the impact of journey on consciousness and conceptions of selfhood. Despite its dubious scientific aims, the Thayer Expedition did play a pivotal role in marking the professional dénouement of Agassiz and the professional rise of William James, bringing together the decline of a nineteenth-century way of looking at personhood as a classifiable category of fixed traits, and a twentieth-century way of looking at it as an unquantifiable, shifting register of action and change. For the twenty-three-year-old James, this realization was especially personal, as his own understandings of selfhood and the value of experience changed throughout the journey, in large part due to his warm interactions with local people but also because of a bout with smallpox in the early part of the trip that rendered him temporarily blind, nearly threatening to end his journey before it truly began, and subsequently changing his perspective on the trip as a whole.

James's experiences in Brazil are best contextualized through a broader understanding of the project of scientific study and travel in the mid-nineteenth century onward, and of Agassiz's own goals for the expedition. As discussed in chapter 1, burgeoning scientific interests throughout the eighteenth and nineteenth centuries all emerged from and worked in favor of empire and nation, from their very arguments to the contrary to their very methods of investigation. The collection and classification of species, the study of disease transmission, and, of course, the tracking of racial differences were each dependent, in various degrees, on the act of *capture*. These "anti-conquerors," whether on a private voyage or a royal commission, branded nature in an attempt to bring or restore European order to the untamed, chaotic splendor of the wild and to protect Empire from its taint. As historian of science Nancy Stepan explains: "By contrasting the scenery, animals, plants, and people at hand with those far away, naturalists instructed and confirmed their readers' sense of European superiority even as they appeared to extol the merits of the foreign. Tropical nature was, in this sense, part of the formation of Europe's identity as a place of temperateness, control, hard work and thriftiness as opposed to the

Figure 2.1. William James in Brazil, 1865. Reproduced with permission from the Houghton Library, Harvard University.

humidity, heat, extravagance and superfluity of the Torrid Zone."[13] The tropics had become, by the mid-nineteenth century, an active European laboratory for ethnological thought.

It was here, in the racially diverse Torrid Zone of 1865 Brazil, that Swiss-American naturalist Louis Agassiz—leading opponent of Darwin's theory in the States—set up an *actual* laboratory in Manaus, the Bureau d'Anthropologie. The bureau's main purpose was to record gradations of difference between "pure" races (which had been photographed in Rio de Janeiro) and "mixed" racial types in Manaus, in order to undo the evolutionary model of common descent and variation. Agassiz hoped to reveal, instead, the true "fixity" of race as a permanent category. He was convinced that continued interracial crossings over successive generations would inevitably degenerate and dilute the "pure" Anglo-Saxon race to the point of extinction and was thus determined to prove his hypothesis.[14]

Agassiz did not begin his scientific career with any particular interest in the study of human races. His primary research had begun in glacial research and ichthyological classification—studying Brazilian and European species of fish, in fact. Agassiz came to the United States in 1846 to study the geology of North America and to give a series of lectures on his research at the Lowell Institute. Sufficiently impressed by the scientific and economic advantages that a research life in the States could offer, he decided to stay, leaving his estranged, ailing wife, Cecile, and young children, Alexander, Ida, and Pauline, behind in Switzerland. (After his wife succumbed to tuberculosis in 1850, Agassiz did call his children to the States and eventually remarried into a wealthy Boston family.) As he toured the United States, Agassiz grew increasingly interested in the "race problem." After his first encounter with black waiters in Philadelphia, he wrote to his mother of his disgust, explaining how he kept his eyes fixed on them "in order to tell them to keep their distance. And when they put their hideous hand on my plate in order to serve me, I wished I were able to distance myself in order to eat my morsel of bread elsewhere."[15]

This visceral fear of contagion fueled Agassiz's pseudoscientific, nativist project. Agassiz also happened to arrive in Cambridge at the height of U.S. "scientific" interest in theories of racial degeneration. Racial theorists Josiah Nott and George Gliddon, following the work of Samuel George Morton, were at work on their landmark *Types of Mankind* (1854), which supported the polygenist theory that different races belonged to different species. Finding an audience for his own theories, based on their sponsorship and introductions, Agassiz went on lecture tours among slaveholders in the South, emphasizing his belief in the biological distinction between white and black races. Through the encouragement of Nott, Gliddon, and his audiences, Agassiz strengthened his own beliefs in creationism and the separate species of mankind, eventually using this logic of racial separation to forward a pro-abolition platform.[16]

But as Darwin's theory crossed over to the States, on the heels of Agassiz's arrival, the scientific tide began to turn away from the charismatic charm of Agassiz's lectures and increasingly unsustainable theories. By midcentury, on the brink of a postevolutionary, post-Emancipation era, Atlantic world science shifted course, both in its objects of inquiry as well as the kinds of authoritative voices it privileged. The entrepreneurial spirit that had led the sciences in the early part of the century, and that had often privileged lay individuals with a curious penchant for innovation and invention, was replaced with a more unified, professionalized, and nationalist vision of science. In fact, a small subset of scientists (including Agassiz) who had self-deprecatingly dubbed themselves the "Scientific Lazzaroni," after the Neapolitan panhandlers and peddlers of the same name, had sought government recognition and institutional support for nearly a decade before the 1863 formation of the National Academy of Sciences (NAS) by President Lincoln. They advocated for the promotion of a professionalized science practiced by highly trained, university-educated practitioners and researchers.[17]

The founding of the Lawrence Scientific School at Harvard in 1847, where James had trained, was an earlier, private realization of the kinds of public institutions and programs the Lazzaroni hoped to foster and promote on a wider national scale. Lincoln's mandate for the newly minted NAS worked alongside this ideal, binding the goals of scientific endeavor with larger national goals of intellectual advancement, stating that the group "shall, whenever called upon by any department of the Government, examine, experiment, and report upon any subject of science or art."[18] The formation of the National Academy of Sciences thus reaffirmed the conjoined projects of science and nation at a time fraught with racial and cultural anxiety, as evolution, emancipation, anthropology, and immigration all came together in a particularly vexed way in the postbellum United States. The movement of ideas and people through the second half of the nineteenth century would clearly have lasting and profound consequences on national policy and scientific endeavor.

Agassiz did believe, along with his peers-turned-professional rivals like Asa Gray and Charles Darwin, in the work of science as "a collective enterprise." But as Christoph Irmscher has pointed out in his measured portrait of Agassiz's life, work, and ideals, this enterprise was, for Agassiz, "a struggle for the *right* reading of nature." He emphasized the paramount role of scientific inquiry as the central disciplinary and epistemological force of his era: "It cannot be too soon understood," he insisted, "that science is one, and whether we investigate philosophy, theology, history, or physics, we are dealing with the same problem, culminating in the knowledge of ourselves."[19] Yet Agassiz's continued insistence on polygenic theories of racial evolution, in the wake of Darwin's increasingly accepted theories to the contrary, and in the midst of an increasingly professionalized route for science, slowly began to widen the gulf between his beliefs and the new direction of scientific inquiry. Although Agassiz's investment in proving his creationist theories through the degenerative implications of race mixture in Brazil was undoubtedly led by his continued (and increasingly solitary) "struggle" to offer "the right reading of nature," it may have also been part of a parallel desire to assimilate into a legacy of American frontiersmanship, as well as a larger global narrative of scientific travel and adventure. This shared frontierist mentality seems to be the key point of convergence that initially brought the young William James and his elder mentor together as they embarked on their journey. (The rest of their travels together, however, were spent intellectually splintering— albeit, respectfully—from one another.)

Young American men of the elite classes were encouraged to "go west" and make their destinies somewhere along the vast, uncharted frontier, just as European naturalists had embraced an "anti-conquest" model that encouraged adventure and discovery amid nature's infinite splendor. So James and Agassiz, too, wished to join this lineage of naturalists and frontiersmen, to secure their place in a long line of influential travelers.[20] For Agassiz, this rite of passage would have the dual benefit of solidifying his assimilation into an American cultural narrative and linking his own fact-finding journey to the exploratory wanderings of Darwin and Humboldt. In fact, while his Brazilian expedition remains the journey for which Agassiz is notoriously (and nefariously) remembered, it is worth noting that he did also complete, toward the end of his life, a deep-sea dredging expedition through South America aboard the *Hassler* in 1871–72, sailing from Boston to Barbados, then down along the South American coast, anchoring in the Straits of Magellan before heading west to San Francisco by way of the Galapagos Islands. It is "oddly fitting," confirms Irmscher, "that the final grand act" of Agassiz's professional life "should be framed as a recasting of the first act of Charles Darwin's career."[21] While that final journey may have marked the culmination of this desire in Agassiz, it was nevertheless first realized by this earlier expedition.

This initial journey, for both Agassiz and James, offered thus a kind of redemption, fulfilling in each a military or scientific *manqué*—a desire to replicate the risks, depredations, and separation endured by soldiers (and in James's case, his younger brothers) in the Civil War; a professional goal to join the proud lineage of explorers and naturalists, from Magellan to Humboldt, who had crossed the ocean, basked in the tropics, had tamed and named the uncharted "wilderness," and returned home to write and retire in infamous glory. The reality of illness and faulty research did not exactly cohere with the grand utopian romance imagined by both men as they embarked on their journey on April 1, 1865, but it certainly changed them both and does still exemplify, in important ways, the limits and possibilities of both scientific investigation and self-knowledge—even if in large part as a cautionary tale.[22]

Thus in 1865, funded by Boston entrepreneur Nathaniel Thayer II, Agassiz assembled a team of fellow naturalists from the Museum of Comparative Zoology to form the Thayer Expedition. His young student collector, William James, also signed on to the journey, eager to learn from his mentor despite their difference of opinion on the evolution question.

The primary aim of the Thayer Expedition was to study the effect of glacial action in South America; its secondary (and independent) aim, to study the effects of race mixture. In addition to these scientific and anthropological experiments, Agassiz also went to advance some of the political and commercial interests of his adoptive country. As historian Maria H. P. T. Machado outlines: "First, the expedition coincided with US pressures on the Brazilian imperial government to open the Amazon to free navigation; second, it took place at a time when some American diplomats and entrepreneurs entertained the idea of resettling recently freed slaves as colonists or apprentices in the Amazon." Aware of Agassiz's friendly epistolary exchanges with Brazilian emperor Pedro II, the U.S. government gave the Thayer Expedition its official support in the hope that Agassiz might use his friendship as leverage to advance U.S. interests. With the help of this official support, along with Agassiz's well-known charisma and his friendship with Dom Pedro II, he was able to persuade the Brazilian government to open the Amazon to foreign navigation.[23]

Agassiz was, of course, less successful in his aims of resettling African Americans along the Amazon. But one of the main purposes of setting

Figure 2.2. Members of Thayer Expedition, 1865. *Sitting on floor, bottom left*: William James; *on chairs, left to right*: D. Bourget, Walter Hunnewell, Jacques Burkhardt, Newton Dexter; *standing, left to right*: Stephen van Rensselaer Thayer, João Martins da Silva Coutinho. Copyright Ernst Mayr Library of the Museum of Comparative Zoology, Harvard University. Reproduced with permission.

up a sustained racial study in the tropics, as the Bureau d'Anthropologie sought to do, was to try to prove that African races were best suited for tropical zones, perhaps thereby strengthening the case for their repatriation in the Amazon region.

This project was a kind of philanthropic addendum to the tenets of racial homogeneity, containment, and nationalism that shaped the Free Soil movement of the 1840s and 1850s. Gaining momentum shortly after Agassiz arrived in the United States in 1846 (and supported initially and primarily by northerners, who did not rely on African slave labor for their economic livelihood), members of the Free Soil Party defended abolition on the grounds that a strong nation was dependent on racial purity. As a result they advocated either the containment of African Americans to the southern United States, or the (second) forced resettlement of African Americans to the tropical countries of South America.[24]

Of course, the idea of "repatriation" had accompanied nativist ideals for the better part of the century (and longer), but as the Civil War brought the reality of a freed, ex-slave population home to racist northerners and southerners alike, the transfer of African Americans to the tropics—primarily to Brazil—became a ready solution to "the race problem," although it had to be presented under the guise of philanthropy and science. Scientists like Agassiz thus argued that the darker races were constitutionally, biologically suited for tropical areas and would thrive there, whereas the lighter races could survive only in temperate regions. The Thayer Expedition and its Bureau d'Anthropologie set out, in part, to provide material evidence to strengthen this claim, and to return with a scientific argument for racial segregation and containment.[25]

Agassiz did this by capitalizing on the emerging technology of photography: He sought to bring home a visual archive of racial degeneration. Instead, what emerges in these photographs is a fascinating representative sample of Brazil's racially diverse population. As scholars like Nicole Fleetwood and Nicholas Mirzoeff have argued, "the photographic 'indexicality of race' grew in importance after the abolition of slavery," as technologies like photography developed alongside a modernizing and expanding visual culture in the late nineteenth century, one that also highlighted racial difference through public events like World's Fairs, museum exhibits, and freak shows. All of these became important tools for capturing and cataloguing difference. This mobile, visual archive of difference took center stage just as Darwin's theories of organic continuity forced readers, scientists, and citizens to rethink boundaries of kinship and community.[26]

Agassiz had a local photographer, German-Brazilian Augusto Stahl, take pictures of the "pure" Africans living in Rio, and then later enlisted Walter Hunnewell, a member of his own Thayer Expedition, to take the photos of the "hybrid" Amazonians in Manaus for comparison. These photos—especially those taken by Stahl, who was renowned throughout Brazil for his experimental and empathetic style—leave viewers wondering whether the photographer's vision is at odds with that of Agassiz. For example, the photo below, of a woman referred to as *Mina Tapa* from the "pure race" series, reveals a woman with a powerful stare and a heavily scarred face and chest. She also wears on her shoulder a *pano da costa* shawl, which had special significance in Afro-Brazilian culture as marking the spiritual leaders of slave communities.[27] The woman's hair is also

Figure 2.3. Tapa Mina, phrenological portrait by Augusto Stahl, glass plate collodion, Rio de Janeiro, ca. 1865. Louis Agassiz Photographic Collection, Pure Race Series. Reproduced with permission from the Peabody Museum of Archaeology & Ethnography, Harvard University.

covered by a silk African turban, or *torço*. This hardly reads as a scientific daguerreotype. Even if that was its photographic purpose, its narrative function does something else: full of ethnic particularity and an expressive gaze that speaks *back* to the viewer, this artifact rejects Agassiz's fantasy of scientific inferiority or even "racial purity." We do not know by what terms this subject has been deemed "pure" African, or how she might self-identify. But she bears the marks, on her clothing and on her skin, of a diasporic, transnational narrative that speaks beyond the photographic frame.[28]

In the Hunnewell series, we see even more clearly the attention to sartorial detail and adornment in both the men and women. Sometimes dressed and sometimes stripped to the waist but for beautiful necklaces, headdresses, or formal slips that remain, the shame is compounded for viewer, sitter, and photographer alike, as the very indignity of the request to disrobe is very much alive in what remains *on* in the photograph.

As Nancy Stepan has shown in her detailed explication of the Manaus photographs, "it is clear from the context, and from the images themselves, that all of these photographs are of *cabaclos*—that is, acculturated men and women from Manaus. . . . They were hardly forest Amerindians, but rather people who ordinarily wore clothes and were now being asked to take them off."[29] Agassiz was obviously unable to prove his radical and scientifically unfounded theory of racial degeneration through these photographs. Other than a memoir, *A Journey in Brazil*, written primarily by his second wife, Elizabeth Agassiz, his ethnological research did not reach a wider audience in its time, instead further splintering Agassiz from the new, evolutionist direction of his scientific community.

Elizabeth, who served as Agassiz's chief scribe on this journey as well as the subsequent *Hassler* expedition, in fact may have—intentionally or not—toned down the potential embarrassment of her husband's "findings" by highlighting the performative nature of his overall enterprise, interspersing her own narrative observations and tidy descriptions of the scenery and people alongside ventriloquized statements by her husband about soil and rock formations, and specimens collected from various sites. As James himself noted in his diary, Mrs. Agassiz "seems to fancy that we are mere figures walking about in strange costume on a stage with appropriate scenery."[30] Like Darwin's playful imagining of himself as "a grand barbarian" (as discussed in chapter 1), and like Franz Boas's unintentional pose of village doctor (as discussed in chapter 3), Elizabeth

Figure 2.4. Portrait of a racial type, unidentified woman, Walter Hunnewell, Manaus, 1865–66. Louis Agassiz Photographic Collection, Mixed Race Series. Reproduced with permission from the Peabody Museum of Archaeology & Ethnography, Harvard University.

Figure 2.5. Portrait of a racial type, unidentified woman, Walter Hunnewell, Manaus, 1865–66. Louis Agassiz Photographic Collection, Mixed Race Series. Reproduced with permission from the Peabody Museum of Archaeology & Ethnography, Harvard University.

Agassiz also performed, through her narrative complement to this photographic archive, the collective and the constructed nature of all scientific endeavor, in which professional and amateur acts of observation and
encounter are necessarily intertwined, blurring the very idea of the disciplining, authoritative gaze.

There is yet a broader racial lesson to emerge from this radical photographic experiment—one that also reveals, like Elizabeth Agassiz's prose,
the impossibility of fixed order beyond the orchestration of narrative.
These photos not only illustrate how rampant and utterly unquantifiable
the study of race mixture was in Brazil but also hint at the comparative
lack of surveillance and legislation of such manufactured difference,
unlike the draconian practices of detecting, policing, and segregating different races in the United States. In a country where slavery still flour-
ished, race mixture was not just an accepted consequence of interracial
contact but a fusion increasingly encouraged and touted by the Brazilian
elite as one of the country's most original features—the convergence of
the African, the AmerIndian, the European, and the Asian in a single
and uniquely New World stock. Racial amalgamation was not considered
degenerative but foundational to the prosperity of the Brazilian nation.[31]

The roots of Brazil's celebratory narrative, however, were of course
embedded in similar fears of blackness and rampant racism among the
Brazilians themselves. Its national resolution lay not in segregation or in
expatriation but in the highly problematic idea of erasure through repro-
duction. Rio's French ambassador, the controversial racialist Joseph-
Arthur de Gobineau, had convinced Dom Pedro II to bring in more
Italians and Germans to work Brazilian plantations in an attempt to dis-
solve the black race from its population. However, toward the end of the
nineteenth century and beyond, Brazilian elites continued to emphasize
the importance of *all* races to the national-racial character. In such a pro-
jection, lauded by other turn-of-the-century Brazilian writers and theorists like Silvio Romero, Brazil's black citizens would play a vital role in
the future of a strong and representative Brazil—a model of geographic
diversity, a literal embodiment of the strengths of the New World.[32]

Instead of a country in decline, and despite its continued practice of
slavery that would extend well toward the end of the century, the Brazil
that Agassiz encountered was not the Brazil of earlier European travelers like Humboldt.[33] It was, as scholar Cannon Schmitt has described, "at
once 'new' and 'old,' open to exploration but already traveled."[34] No longer
in search for the beginnings of civilization and humanity, Louis Agassiz

came to this same place to unearth the only mystery he felt was left to be unraveled—the end of civilization and humanity. Instead, what he found was a nation on the brink of modernity, suffused with the same racial tensions as those in *his* new world of North America, but supplanting that tension not with theories of degeneration but of regeneration.

The difference at the heart of these two nationalist visions is hardly congratulatory for either country. The propagation of Brazil's own myth as a melting pot of racial fusion is unconvincing for a nation that did not abolish slavery until 1888.[35] But the significance of this kind of rhetoric and promotion of race mixture, especially in such a scientifically and politically fraught moment, stands as an important example of how narratives of racial performance began to supplant narratives of racial order. Unlike traditional narratives of descent, which are concerned with tracing, discovering, and distinguishing past origins in order to situate the present organic structure, the model of diasporic personhood performed and recognized in Brazil (with all its attendant problems and contradictions) reveals itself to be uncontainable and resistant to classification. It thus destabilizes and extends our understanding of ontology as both deeply rooted in the body and also untethered from the category of individual subject, representing an indissoluble collectivity—an accumulating discourse of and beyond the body that is always moving, becoming, and unbecoming.

William James began his Thayer Expedition journey with all the attendant expectations of a young man who had read many a romantic and orientalist adventure tale. Although his time in Brazil exists primarily as an epistolary record, along with a few sketches and journal entries, a closer examination of these scattered glimpses provides not only a different point of entry into Agassiz's mission but also reveals the impact of these early travels on the eventual career and influence of William James on a new era of scientific and cultural thought.

An early letter to his family conveys James's conventional style of travel narrative, as he writes dramatically yet typically in April 1865, upon the *Colorado*'s approach to the Rio de Janeiro harbor, that "no words of mind, or of any man short of Williams the divine can give any idea of magnificence of this harbor & its approaches. The boldest grandest mountains, far and near, the palms and other trees of such vivid green as I never saw any where else." He continues with further confirmation that all appears as statically blissful as he had imagined: "The town," he writes, "realizes my idea of an African town in its architecture and effect. Almost everyone is a negro or a negress, which words I perceive we don't know the meaning of with us; a great many of them are native Africans & tattooed. The men have white linen drawers and short shirts. . . . The women wear huge turbans and have a peculiar rolling gait. . . . Their attitudes as they sleep & lie about the streets are picturesque to the last degree."[36] Espousing a typical imperialist vision of tropical splendor, in which a Western-conjured image of otherness is mirrored back for his consumption in a familiar yet inspirational way, James is nonetheless careful to point to the difference between *these* "negros" and those "we don't know the meaning of" back home. Although his wording in this passage is somewhat subtle, his implication suggests an initial acceptance of surface-based notions of racial essence: dress, gait, physical markings are constitutive, at least from afar, of these residents of Rio as *native* Africans, and the "purity" of their Africanness makes them a "picturesque" part of the local scenery, unlike the African Americans at home.

These early musings seem to align most directly with Agassiz's vision of fixed racial traits, and the young James is initially smitten with the charisma of his mentor, as were many in Agassiz's circle. James writes in the same letter home that "Agassiz is one of the most fascinating men personally that I ever saw. I could listen to him talk by the hour." He adds, however, a hint of the shift to come, concluding that "he is so childlike."[37] It takes only a month into the journey for James's professional opinion of the man to sour a bit, even as he remains taken with his personal charms, writing that Agassiz's "charlatanerie is almost as great as his solid worth; and it seems of an unconscious childish kind that you can't condemn him for as you would most people. He wishes to be too omniscient. But his personal fascination is very remarkable."[38] As James's disillusion grows, his depictions of tropical splendor are interspersed, in his letters home, with an expression of his desire to come home. "I think that I shall probably return home after the end of this journey, if I make it without going to the Amazons," writes James to his father in June. "I shall have seen enough on the journey. Since seeing more of Agassiz, my desire to be with him, so as to learn from him has much diminished. He is doubtless a man of some wonderful mental faculties, but such a politician & so self-seeking & illiberal to others that it sadly diminishes one's respect for him."[39]

Perhaps an offshoot of his discomfort with Agassiz's vision for the expedition, and of his clandestine photographic experiments (though James makes no direct mention of these in his letters home), James also develops an overall disdain for the act of collection and categorization, which was his primary occupation on the journey. Again, in his June letter to his father, Henry Sr., the young man complains that "I find that by staying I shall learn next to nothing of Natural History as I care about learning it. My whole work will be mechanical, finding objects and packing them, and working so hard at that and in travelling that no time at all will be found for studying their structures. The affair reduces itself thus to so many months spent in physical exercise."[40] His frustration leads to an early realization that "I am cut out for a speculative rather than an active life." James distances himself from the great heroes of empire and travel literature, admitting to his father that "on the steamer I began to read Humboldt's *Travels*. Hardly had I opened the book when I seemed to become illuminated. Good Heavens! When such men are provided to do the work of traveling, exploring and observing for humanity, men who gravitate into their works as the air does into our lungs, what need, what *business* have *we* outsiders to pant after them and toilsomely try to serve as their substitutes?"[41]

James's desire for a more contemplative way of studying the natural world is fulfilled in the most unforeseen and unlikely way, just a few months into his journey: through his temporary condition of blindness. Rather than cut his journey short, as he had originally planned, James's recovery and renewed vision instill in him a completely different perspective on his role in the expedition, and his relationship with the people he meets along the way.

Although his bout with blindness is somewhat brief, the worst of it lasting from mid-June to mid-July (though his eyes remained weak for some time after that), the slow return of vision as experience in itself allows James to "feel like a new being" and to participate in his journey in a different way than the standard scientific observer.[42] Although his language is still firmly situated within the tradition of imperial wonder akin to Humboldt, Darwin, Hudson, and other naturalists who also experienced and narrated their journeys of the natural world in the awe-inspired prose of museum-goers staring at a landscape painting of the primordial past, James seems to internalize the space in a very presentist way that alters his narration from a strictly panoramic view-from-the-harbor style of writing often employed by other scientists and ethnographers of his time (and by James himself in his earliest depiction above). James's writing, as his journey progresses, betrays a more impressionistic, if still imperial and fetishistic, quality, as evidenced in a letter he writes to his brother Henry in July, as his sight slowly returns.

Although he begins the missive with a similar expression of inarticulable awe as he did in his earliest letter home, and although he ends with an aerial, imperial glance across the landscape, he also inserts himself more fully into the chaos that is, for the first time, too overwhelming to order and name. As his vision returns, James writes more earnestly from within the realm of experience, not the distant horizon of observation:

> No words, but only savage inarticulate cries can express the gorgeous love-liness of the walk I have been taking. Houp la la! The bewildering profu-sion & confusion of the vegetation, the inexhaustible variety of its forms & tints (yet they tell us we are in the winter when much of its brilliancy is lost) are *literally* such as you have never dreamt of. The brilliancy of the sky and the clouds, the effect of the atmosphere which gives their proportional distance to the diverse planes of the landscape make you admire the Old Gal nature.[43]

James also writes in August to his mother about "the jumping toothache" he feels in his eyes if he sets his sights too long upon an object, intimating through a language of hunger and consumption that his desire to devour and feast upon this wondrous repast of nature is curbed by a reflexive resistance to prolonged study—a consequence of his physical limits, to be sure, but one that shapes his re-visions of Brazil, in any case. Unlike his elder counterpart, Darwin, on *his* first journey abroad, whose language and observations grew increasingly focused as his journey progressed, James's language and (in)sights grow increasingly undisciplined and wan-dering, taking in the scenery and the people in a manner that is less impe-rial and more delighted by acts of unlearning.[44]

As his vision and his health improve, and as "the real enjoyment of the expedition is beginning & I am tasting the sweets of these lovely forests here," James writes to his mother, "I find it impossible," after all, "to tear myself away & this morning I told Prof. that I would see this Amazon trip through at any rate."[45] James's encounters with local people, from boat-men to servants, allow him to see and accept this world on its own terms. By the time he is ready to leave the expedition, James begins to see him-self—in a step beyond Darwin's amused sense of his costumed self as "a grand barbarian"—as part of the local culture. By the end of his journey, he sleeps in a hammock, speaks rudimentary Portuguese, and refers teas-ingly to his baby sister as "the lovely white child" that he, "the red man of the forest" would "like to hug" and hold close.[46]

In his eight-month stint in Brazil, James learned not only that he was more suited for philosophy than science but also, as Darwin did to some degree, some valuable lessons about the cloak of cultural difference. As his tone shifts and matures throughout his journey, James reserves most of his imperial awe for the landscape, discussing people and places through relative comparisons that make them seem more relatable to his reading audience: his family at home in Cambridge. James thwarts the more exotic descriptions in favor of depictions of the Amazon and its inhabitants that are more familiar than foreign. He writes, for example, that the "streets and shops" of Rio "remind you so much of Europe" and that there is a kind of monotony and tedium in tropical nature, as there would be in a stretch of American or British wilderness.[47] He also writes of an Indian woman he meets: "I marveled, as I always do, at the quiet urbane polite tone of the conversation between my friends and the old lady. Is it race or is it circumstance that makes these people so refined and well bred? No gentleman of Europe has better manners and these are peasants."[48] Of course, some of James's letters are also riddled with his share of negative stereotypes about "lazy" and intellectually "barren" Brazilians and Indians, as well as an "amusing" anecdote about the temporary kidnapping of a seemingly willing young Indian boy when labor was needed.[49] But overall, James found far more continuities than differences and felt an increasing sense of shame at his mentor's treatment of the local people at the Bureau d'Anthropologie. Although James never took a public stand against Agassiz, he is perhaps the only expedition member to write anything about the experiments or the local community's reaction to them. In a November 10 diary entry, James writes of his presence at a photographic session where prominent Brazilian politician Tavares Bastos came in and mocked the enterprise:

On entering the room found Prof. engaged in cajoling 3 moças whom he called pure Indians but who, I thought as afterward appeared, had white blood. They were very nicely dressed in white muslin & jewelry with flowers in their hair & an excellent smell of pripioca. Apparently refined, at all events not sluttish, they consented in the utmost liberties being taken with them and two without much trouble were induced to strip and pose naked. While we were there, Sr. Tavares Bastos came in and asked me mocking if I was attached to the Bureau d'Anthropologie.[50]

James seems to share the politician's tongue-in-cheek sensibility about this pseudoprofessional enterprise, and questions the racial constitution of the women Agassiz had photographed as "pure"-blooded Indians. It is clear that James did not participate in the "collection" of specimen for this portion of Agassiz's journey, and that his most important revelations came from his own interactions with people in Brazil.

On the whole, however, I would argue that James's most profound lesson on this journey is an introspective, or transpersonal one. His firsthand experience with actual blindness in a foreign land, coupled with his early disillusion with Agassiz, provide him with a particular insight, or second sight, for the rest of his journey into the limits of truth, self-knowledge, and the knowledge of others. As a result, he learns from his own personal experience how scientific and cultural blindness operate—the limits of what one chooses to see and ignore, both in oneself and others. James expresses this vexed relationship between insight and blindness in his final letter home to his mother, in which he writes of his current inability to envision life as he once knew it in Boston, and how this same feeling will soon apply to the time he has spent in Brazil. His voice shifts back and forth between these two visions and desires: of current satiation and a longing to return home, followed by the worry that he will be estranged from the life that awaits him there, and that his visions of this space will soon fade:

> I am on the whole very glad this thing is winding up—not that I have not enjoyed parts of it intensely and regard it as one of the best spent portions of my life; but enough is as good as a feast; I thoroughly *hate* collecting, and long to be back to books, studies &c after this elementary existence. You have no idea, my dearest Mother, how strange that home life seems to me from the depths of this world buried as it is in mere vegetation and physical needs & enjoyments. I hardly think you will be able to understand me, but the idea of the people swarming about as they do at home, killing themselves with thinking about things that have no connexion with their merely external circumstances, studying themselves into fevers, going mad about religion, philosophy, love & sich [*sic*] . . . seems almost incredible and imaginary, and yet I only left it 8 months ago. . . . I dare say when I get home I shall have for a time many a pang of nostalgia for this placid Arcadia; even now it often suffices for me to see an orange tree or one of these mellow sunsets to make me shrink from the thought of giving them up all together. At one time this was so strong that I could hardly bear to think of not going back to the superb old Rio with the Prof. and revis[it]ing all those places on the coast which I could enjoy so little when we passed them, owing to my eye.[51]

Although James's double vision is still one that conventionally pits society against nature in a typically dangerous dualism, there is yet a seed here of his future research into psychic duality, and the ways in which a person can be at once home and elsewhere, and can have warring desires, memories, and affiliations in a single body. This journey into the Amazon and into himself shaped James's later work on consciousness, work that would have a lasting influence on philosophical and literary articulations of the experience of raced personhood in the new century.

James returned to the United States plagued with continued eye strain and severe depression. Despite his struggles, he completed his medical studies in 1869, though he never became a practicing physician. Instead, he accepted a series of appointments to teach at Harvard that spanned a wide range of interrelated fields across the next decade, starting out first in anatomy and physiology, then moving to psychology, and eventually splitting his time between philosophy and psychology.

It is during this first decade of his career that James first experimented with nitrous oxide. Introduced to it by an eccentric New York philosopher and pamphleteer named Benjamin Paul Blood, James became intrigued by the challenge of "getting behind" the self as a means of plumbing the depths of one's own consciousness and tried (unsuccessfully) to use nitrous oxide to help carry him over.[52]

Although this is a period of James's own career that is often glossed over, since his rambling "findings" while under the influence tend not to be as illuminating as the experience itself (which gets us to the gulf between experience and the language of observation once more), it serves, nonetheless, as an important illustration of how science began to intervene in questions of the self that had, until this point, been left to philosophers and clergymen. The desire to utilize the methods of scientific excavation to evoke the romantic mysteries of the self provided a new angle to a broader nineteenth-century transcendentalism, in which the hand of God revealed itself through Nature's divine beauty. By the latter half of the nineteenth century, science had joined that mission, asserting itself "as a sort of natural theology placed at the service of mankind."[53]

James's work on theories of consciousness continued well past this era, of course. In 1884, he became a founding member of the American chapter of the British Society for Psychical Research, which made "an organized and systematic attempt" to study "that large group of debatable phenomena designated by such terms as 'mesmeric,' 'psychical,' and 'spiritualistic.'"[54]

James hoped to expand the realm of scientific inquiry into this uncharted territory, in part to skew the dividing line between the material and the spiritual, or what he referred to as the tension between the "scientific-rational" mind and the "feminine-mystical" mind. By opening up scientific inquiry in this way to make space for the unknown and for the consideration of the personality biases that a scientist brings to his own research, James was able to use his new way of looking—simultaneously inward and outward—to level a critique against the positivist era of the omniscient scientist. Whether or not James's theories emerged from his romantic experiences of second sight in Brazil or from his negative experiences with Agassizian positivism in this same space, it is clear that the Thayer Expedition played no small part in the shaping of an oppositional discourse that would have profound political implications for scientists and race scholars working at the boundaries of the scientific and the spiritual in the new century.[55]

In a passage from his 1909 "Confidences of a Psychic Researcher," in which he writes about the transpersonal connections hidden within the self, James illustrates how his brand of rhizomatic thinking about consciousness might easily translate into a broader political vision of the buried, connected histories of the wider Atlantic world:

> Out of my experience . . . one fixed conclusion dogmatically emerges, and that is, that we with our lives are like islands in the sea, or like trees in the forest. The maple and the pine may whisper to each other with their leaves, and Conanicut and Newport hear each other's foghorns. But the trees also commingle their roots in the darkness underground, and the islands also hang together through the ocean's bottom. Just so there is a continuum of cosmic consciousness, against which our individuality builds but accidental fences, and onto which our several minds plunge as into a mother-sea or reservoir. Our "normal" consciousness is circumscribed for adaptation to our external earthly environment, but the fence is weak in spots, and fitful influences from beyond leak in, showing the otherwise unverifiable common connexion.[56]

James provides, once more, a poetic rendering of personhood as a multilayered self, a "continuum of cosmic consciousness" that is protected and hidden away by the "accidental fences" of public persona. The individuality we must present to the world in order to be properly read and translated can only skim the surface of ontology. The inaccessible "truth" of experience must give way to the very limited and dangerously fallible "truth" of observation. James's exploration into the limits of scientific inquiry, from his earliest realizations in the Bureau d'Anthropologie to his larger explorations into the unconscious and the mystical (that went far beyond these early experiments with psychedelic drugs, of course, to span an illustrious career as a pioneering figure in psychology), did expand the boundaries of scientific study from the conventional field of symptoms and objects to a larger field that encompassed the transpersonal and mystical, as well as the transhistorical and communal.

It is through this transition in late-nineteenth-century thought that we begin to see an avenue for a discourse of racial consciousness and personhood that emerges *through* science, not in spite of it. Just as scholars like James made room for the inclusion of the unconscious and the mystical in scientific discourse, African American scholars used it to critique scientific positivism, conceptualizing "the social scientist as a disunified and subjective observer in contradiction to the confidently unitary ideal self of the Victorian social investigator."[57] African American scholars and scientists like Frederick Douglass and Martin Delany were already at work on ideas of racial consciousness and social and historical continuities in the decades preceding James's rise to scientific notoriety. Martin Delany might have even become a central figure in the life and education of the young James had he been allowed to continue his own education at Harvard Medical School in the 1850s. But the public outcry that erupted over the arrival of Delany and two other students, as the first three African American students admitted, led to their prompt dismissal and to Delany's subsequent career-shaping turn to black nationalism and a desire to repatriate his people to Liberia. It was the advancement of his own ethnological ideas about the superiority of the black race, as outlined in his 1879 *Principia of Ethnology: The Origin of Races and Color*, that serves as a powerful rejoinder to Agassiz, Norton, Gliddon, and the rest and that originally sutured the scientific and the spiritual together, citing "classical and Biblical sources" to situate Africa as the birthplace of intellectual and scientific innovation erroneously attributed to the West.[58]

At the turn of the century, though, it was a young W. E. B. Du Bois who first learned of Jamesian ideas of consciousness as a student at Harvard himself from 1888 to 1892. Du Bois writes that it was James who led him "out of the sterilities of scholastic philosophy to realist pragmatism."[59] By the time Du Bois developed the notion of double consciousness, the term "already had wide currency in the late nineteenth century as a name for the phenomenon of multiple personality."[60] But both Du Bois and James worked, throughout their careers, to detach the stigma of pathology from the notion of double consciousness. For Du Bois, this had particularly important consequences for questions of race, as he already understood the clinical and pathologizing implications of the term "Negro Problem," thus opening his discussion of *The Souls of Black Folk* with that well-known rhetorical, "How does it feel to be a problem?"[61] The very question itself hints at pathology and the need for an "official" investigation.[62]

Both men worked, instead, at the interstices of science and mysticism, to "make intelligible that which has been relegated to the outside of normative cultural boundaries" and to envision the permeability of the self as a gift, not a pathology. For both men, the solution rested, in large part, on the ownership and direction of one's vision—the harnessing of a "second sight" that allowed one to step outside oneself and maintain both a scientific invisibility and a mystical insight into "unmediated truth." The veil, in Du Bois, then, is not an accidental fence or defense mechanism that represses the self but a protective gift that allows omniscient power and strategic camouflage. Thus the key to activating racial consciousness is to transform what seems to be a curse of repression and blindness into the transpersonal gift of second sight—a double consciousness—which has been in one's possession since birth but must be awakened and harnessed in order to effect real change.

It is important to note that this vision is more fluid than syncretic—it is not offered in either Jamesian or Du Boisian philosophy as a compartmentalization of the selves, which could be read as a curative or transcendent ideal. Rather, "the figure of double consciousness" embraces multiplicity in an empowering, self-actualized way and "represents an alternative subject position to that constructed by western science." Like James's own experiences with blindness and Du Bois's own experiences behind the veil, self-knowledge, for both thinkers, comes *through* materiality and kinship. Again, the spiritual and the scientific, in this context, are linked to embodied history and shared experience, not to the passive spectatorship of positivism.[63] James highlights the importance of blurring disciplinary boundaries (and institutions) in order to unleash the complexities of the mind, stating, in 1901, that "the menagerie and the madhouse, the nursery, the prison, and the hospital, have been made to deliver up their material. The world of the mind is shown as something infinitely more complex than was suspected; and whatever beauties it may still possess, it has lost at any rate the beauty of academic neatness."[64]

These abstract concepts of consciousness, vision, and racial performance come to life in the fiction of turn-of-the-century writer Pauline Hopkins, who takes this chapter's concerns with science, race, and transpersonal journeying to a vital space in the history of African American consciousness, especially at the turn of the twentieth century: Ethiopia. Hopkins's vision, as portrayed in her 1902–3 serialized novel *Of One Blood: Or, the Hidden Self*, brings together Delany's own work on Ethiopia as the ancient source of Western modernity and his firm political advocacy of African return, James's scientific investigations into the "unclassified residuum" of the self, and Du Bois's brilliant dictum of an African American double consciousness in which observation and experience, nation and race, come together in a joint call for both introspection and political action. The convergence of these ideas would transform the study of racial lineage and racial consciousness from the realm of cultural curiosity and scientific pathology to a model of political possibility for the new century.

Hopkins's novel propels us forward to the turn of the century, to a post–Reconstruction era U.S. landscape in which the racial paranoia that fueled Agassiz's Brazilian mission was kept alive through the legislated separation of races via *Plessy v. Ferguson* (1896). The terror of the auction block was replaced with the terror of the lynch mob, and the terms of inclusion or exclusion from the national narrative often depended on the detection of color. The story centers on the character of Reuel Briggs, a mixed-race African American man with a gift/curse of mesmeric power, who is passing as white in order to complete his studies unimpeded at Harvard Medical School.[65] After a series of misadventures, Reuel finds himself on an archaeological expedition to Africa, arranged by his alleged best friend, Aubrey Livingstone. It is here that Reuel discovers—through mesmeric visions—that Aubrey not only arranged this trip as an assassination plot to have Reuel killed abroad and to destroy his (thankfully, unconsummated) marriage to the lovely Dianthe Lusk, but that they are *all* siblings by blood. Born to a slave mother and slave-owning father, the children had been separated at birth, and only Aubrey had been raised as legitimate heir to their white father's fortune. The novel tidily resolves the sins of incest with the death of Aubrey and Dianthe and restores the pride of kinship with Reuel's discovery, during his expedition, that he is heir to the throne of Telassar, a hidden, thriving civilization in Ethiopia, and that he is betrothed to the beautiful African queen Candace, who conveniently bears a striking resemblance to his dear, lost Dianthe.

Reuel is introduced to readers as a studious young man, isolated by the secret of his racial identity and supernatural powers, contemplating suicide while reading *The Unclassified Residuum*, a fictive book attributed to Alfred Binet (whose actual 1890 work, *On Double Consciousness*, along with the work of William James, as discussed, had a striking influence on Du Bois's subsequent formulation of this idea). However, as scholars have noted, the passages excerpted in Hopkins's novel about occult practices of healing, and the "effects of the imagination," come not from Binet but from an essay written by William James, also in 1890, entitled "The Hidden Self" (which is also Hopkins's subtitle for this novel), in which he writes:

> No part of the unclassified residuum [of human experience] has usually been treated with a more contemptuous scientific disregard than the mass of phenomena generally called *mystical*. Physiology will have nothing to do with them. Orthodox psychology turns its back on them. Medicine sweeps them out; or, at most, when in an anecdotal vein, records a few of them as "effects of the imagination"—a phrase of mere dismissal, whose meaning, in this connection, it is impossible to make precise. All the while, however, the phenomena are there, lying broadcast over the surface of history.[66]

The disciplinary rejection of these mystical phenomena from a science that cordons itself off as a "closed and completed system of truth" thus renders them "unclassifiable," explains James.[67] He then carefully and strategically uses this rejection to expose the man-made nature of accepted scientific truths, scolding that "we college-bred gentry" are smug in our "shock" at occasionally "stumbling upon" *other* kinds of journals whose readers are "not only living and ignoring us and all our gods, but actually reading and writing and cogitating without ever a thought of our canons, standards, and authorities." He thus invites his readers to change course and to insist, instead, on the porosity of scientific boundaries, imploring that we must work together to "renovate" science by reconsidering these "wild facts . . . which threaten to break up the system." This "renewed" science, promises James, will and must include "new formulas" that hold "more of the voice of the exceptions in them than of what were supposed to be the rules."[68] By making room for the wild and undisciplined side of science, by revealing its constructedness and porosity, explain Hopkins scholars like Thomas Otten, "James also seems to validate those moments in black letters in which basic assumptions about identity become open to question."[69]

Hopkins's Reuel is introduced as just such an exceptional character, already mired in these conflicts of scientific and cultural duality. Passing as white, hiding his mesmeric gifts, he is trying to find a space in this borderland between the scientific-rational and the feminine-mystical, between America and Africa. Of course, these dualities are never so clearly demarcated in life as they are in fiction, and Reuel's crisis of identity, in an actual case, would have been far too complicated to resolve with the seamless merging of two clearly defined identities, each easily mapped on a separate continent. Yet, he serves as a symbolic example of global racial and scientific pride at an early political moment for the "New Negro" movement, in which the work of racial uplift and solidarity in the new century would emphasize the dual importance of both black internationalism and black activism. As a composite sketch of Delany, Du Bois, and James, Reuel shares some of their biographical details (as a student at Harvard interested in the occult; as a young man who embarks on a scientific expedition that turns into a narrative of African return), but he also represents their intellectual and political legacy, as he is able to use his own gift of second sight to lead his people to a new future that resolves the dualities raised by James and Du Bois through an African return advocated by Delany. Reuel brings these mystical phenomena to the forefront of scientific and political discourse, and literalizes the experience of pan-Africanism by bringing buried memories and histories to the surface in other characters, as well as channeling these in himself. Reuel thus represents a new era in which the scientific and the spiritual might work together to create a new scientific-mystical global, racial consciousness.[70]

There is, of course, an essential biologism at work in Hopkins's vision, even as she constructs a discourse around blood and purity that stands as a response against racialists of previous decades, like Agassiz, who sought to use that same discourse to promote and prove the degeneration of races through blood mixing. Hopkins instead uses "blood" alternatingly to refer to all peoples of the world (citing the biblical and Darwinian refrain repeatedly throughout the novel: "Of one blood have I made all nations of men to dwell upon the whole face of the earth"), or to those of "pure" African ancestry (like Queen Candace). By using blood to point to these contradictory yet connected categories, Hopkins hints at the impossibility of racial classification, since the lines of descent are not always knowable or traceable.[71]

Because Hopkins's story is as much about the history of a family and a people as it is the story of a single man or woman, her interest in the occult also departs from the mere curiosity of scientists like James and Blood, who used recreational drugs to attempt to "get behind the self." For characters like Reuel and Dianthe, the act of "getting behind the self" is revelatory of a larger history that neither could access without the help of mesmeric intervention that is outside the parameters of conventional scientific discipline.

Although fields like psychology, philosophy, and even archaeology readily incorporated the occult sciences as part of their investigation of "alternative consciousness," Hopkins understood the more serious implications and opportunities of these cross-disciplinary interventions, making brilliant use of their inherent and increasing overlap.

Through the simultaneous invocation of multiple sciences of "the occult, ethnology, and archaeology, as well as psychology," as critics like Susan Gillman have noted, Hopkins "foregrounds the mobility of nineteenth-century sciences as interracial, transcultural meeting grounds." In so doing, she uses the occult to bring racial consciousness to the fore of scientific investigation in a new and restorative way, not as the locus of repressed degeneracy, but as the hidden archive of a stolen prosperity and greatness. The merging of evolutionary thought and occult practice succeeds in Hopkins's work, then, where her "stubborn biologism" fails. For, while Gillman and others, as discussed above, have rightly criticized Hopkins's dangerous reliance on the same pseudoscientific and conservative notions of *blood* as the basis for racial superiority or bland social harmony that eugenicists and evangelists espoused, it is precisely her investment in the occult that extends and moves her "blood talk" beyond monogenesis, evolution, and the biological, and into the realm of a broader, diasporic historical consciousness that resides "behind the self." Through a deliberate crossing of disciplinary fields, Hopkins restores the incontrovertible truth of a racial unity routed through multiple bodies, histories, and most importantly, a shared consciousness that allows (indeed, insists upon) the participation of "all nations" and all disciplines in the reclamation of Africa's past prosperity, and in the prophetic vision of its future success.[72]

To return, then, to the novel's depiction of such crossings, we find that, when Reuel first sees Dianthe in her trance-like state, conventional physicians have pronounced her dead. But Reuel has already had a vision about her and knows he must use a different method to heal her. "How important the knowledge of whither life tends!" thinks Reuel to himself, as he looks upon Dianthe in her suspended state:

> Here is shown the setting free of a *disciplined* spirit giving up its mortality
> for immortality—the condition necessary to know God. Death! There is no

death. Life is everlasting, and from its reality can have no end. Life is real and never changes, but preserves its identity eternally as the angels, and the immortal spirit of man, which are the only realities and continuities in the universe, God being over all, Supreme Ruler and Divine Essence from whom comes all life. Somewhat in this train ran Reuel's thoughts as he stood beside the seeming dead girl, the cynosure of all the medical faculty there assembled.[73]

Reuel's own mesmeric powers are a direct link to James's later work on hypnosis and the unconscious, but his second sight is actually mediated through a more powerful figure who remains in the shadows of the novel, yet is central to all its revelations. This is Mira, the mother of Reuel, Dianthe, and Aubrey, who appears throughout the novel to give prescient advice. She comes and goes as an apparition, visible only to them, to provide clues (and to encourage them, as her name itself commands, to *look*).[74]

Mira is the real visionary of the novel who directs the characters' geographical and even transpersonal movements, and Reuel's second sight seems directed by her in the service of the family. Second sight is a gift passed down through the maternal line and will be used for the noble work of global racial uplift. In this way, Hopkins's use of the occult moves beyond a simple cross-disciplinary desire to merge the scientific and the spiritual, or to pit racial science's blood discourse against itself. Hopkins routes the future of scientific endeavor through a transcontinental family line. We see this not only in the figure of Mira but also in the transparent body of Queen Candace, through which all could see "the blood circulate and from whom life flowed."[75]

Hopkins's vision of a pan-African family is realized not only though the shadowy revelations of Mira but through a larger narrative of mother country and mother guidance that was also a major source of race pride at the turn of the century—Ethiopianism, which was a common element in the rhetoric of many African and African American writers and political leaders in the early part of the twentieth century.[76] Hopkins takes this symbolic affinity with the Ethiopian homeland and resituates it in the body of one of its American sons. The shame of slave descent is replaced with the pride of noble origins, and the dreams of past glory are transformed into a future promise made possible *only* through the transatlantic return. By restoring Reuel in Ethiopia as the rightful leader of a proud race, Hopkins's "Ethiopianist vision explicitly rewrites the evolutionary narrative of reversion to savagery by predicating the prophetic future of the black race directly on its early greatness."[77]

The embrace of Ethiopianism in a novel that brings together science and race allows a re-vision of Africa as a space whose histories also move beyond and outside the practice of slavery. The pride of Ethiopian innovation and strength also revises the racist ethnological vision of scientists and "Egyptologists" like Samuel Morton, Josiah Nott, and George Gliddon of the 1840s and 1850s. The fact that Reuel's own embrace of Ethiopianism occurs on just the kind of naturalist and exploratory journey that was historically undertaken by those who wished to prove the backwardness of Africa is one of the novel's more interesting reversals.

Reuel's expedition first arrives in the panethnic, Arab space of Tripoli before happening upon the isolated, racially "pure" space of Telassar. Represented as both ancient and thriving, Telassar is described as hibernating, waiting for modernity to arrive and guide it into the twentieth century. As much as the novel resists Western stereotypes of Africa as stagnant and backward, Telassar is still presented as a "remnant," a place *out of time*, waiting "behind the protection of our mountains and swamps, secure from the intrusion of a world that has forgotten, for the coming of our king who shall restore to the Ethiopian race its ancient glory."[78] So Telassar lies not in ruin but in a preserved state of anticipation, waiting to be christened (literally) by the bold Western explorer who will claim it as his birthright. But it waits not just for any explorer but for the singular figure of Reuel—the son who holds the birthright of two continents, bearing the best of Africa *and* America in his blood. The fact that Reuel finds his roots *not* on the West African shorelines of the slave trade but in the biblically vital space of Ethiopia is crucial, for not only did the Kushite civilization of Ethiopia precede the rise of European empires, its current Emperor Menelik II and his troops had enjoyed a very recent victory in the 1896 Battle of Adwa, defeating the invading Italians in "the most spectacular setback to European imperialism of its time."[79]

Reuel's expedition might stand as an African American rejoinder to the call that young men should "go west" to find their futures, as discussed earlier. While the American frontier had been deemed generally closed by the start of the new century, it had been unofficially closed to African American men from their arrival on American soil. Yet, the romance of the journey—whether west or abroad, permanent or touristic—still called to all young men of the period. Exposure to the challenges of nature and one's own physical limits was considered, "according to the reigning notion of the masculine ideal," to be vital to the cultivation of character, vigor, and self-reliance, as figures like Theodore Roosevelt proselytized, and scholars like Anthony Rotundo, Kim Townsend, and Gail Bederman have discussed at length.[80]

Reuel's expedition, however, does not fulfill an empty masculinist quest for individualism and conquest but is rather the culmination of his (unconscious) search for kinship and community, a most dramatically literalized rite of passage into king-dom. In navigating new landscapes and buried cultures, Reuel comes to understand that "he is infused with the racial survivals of ancient Africa." This, coupled with his Western scientific training, "leads him back into a mystical transhistorical dimension where he can assume his rightful place in the lineage of deified Ethiopian kings."[81]

Is it possible to consider Reuel Briggs, or King Ergamenes, *rooted* though he is in ancient and biblical tradition, as symbolizing a new Atlantic future, like a scientific Toussaint for the twentieth century? Someone who reclaims the tropical kingdom from the white imperialists, slavers, and naturalists who sought only to possess, destroy, or study it from a distance? How will kinship work in this new space? Will this Atlantic American Adam be subsumed by African culture, and if so, what happens to that *other* legacy—of kinship borne of dispersal, alliance, and struggle? Is it obliterated, in shame, like the names of those who traveled alongside his noble parents?

The captive travelers of the transatlantic slave trade and their kin—whether deemed so by common experience or language, by blood, geography, or legal assignment—performed, through the slipperiness of that very category, the false totality of any master narrative of singular racial unity. For even Reuel and his progeny will carry European and African blood—the future, as the past, is panracial. But by debunking white Western supremacy through and against the bloodline, writers like Hopkins and Delany, among many others, worked from within the parameters of racial science to extricate narratives of raced personhood from fixed legal and scientific determinations.[82]

Though the body, in science, was long considered a rooted object to be studied, sorted, and ranked, its physical and psychic journeys reveal that its histories and continuities were more accurately understood through a tracing of its routes. The cultural, racial, and even transpersonal crossings and remakings—the consequence of centuries of Atlantic journey and encounter—hailed a shift in nineteenth- and twentieth-century understandings of personhood, from biological and legal determinism, to a mobile and resistant cultural and political act.

3

Creole Authenticity and Cultural Performance

Ethnographic Personhood in the Twentieth Century

> It is at their undefinable limits, through "precipitate contact," that cultures move.
>
> Édouard Glissant, *Poetics of Relation*

On Tuesday, December 27, 1831, after nearly a month's delay due to inclement weather, the HMS *Beagle* finally set sail from Plymouth, embarking on what would become its most famous expedition, with the young naturalist Charles Darwin on board. Later that evening, some 4,000 nautical miles west, an initially peaceful slave "labor strike" in the British colony of Jamaica broke into full rebellion, hastening the passage of the 1833 Slavery Abolition Act just over a year later. These parallel events, once again, bind science, personhood, and political action together in a new way in this period, revealing, as I will show in this chapter, how New World encounters and alliances encouraged both the understanding and the assertion of personhood as a practice that precedes and exceeds taxonomies of nation, unravels the premise of racial hierarchy, and productively complicates the study and performance of culture and self in the new century. For as we navigate the second half of this study, we begin to meet travelers who cross more deliberately and strategically the manufactured boundaries between nations, races, cultures, and the professions that observe, study, and define them.

As Britain's largest American slave colony in 1831, Jamaica was a politically and economically vital holding for the Crown, as well as a complex society in which certain "elite" slaves, such as those who worked as personal attendants to their masters, enjoyed some freedom and mobility that allowed them—even if surreptitiously—to access information and organize on their own. As such, when slave laborers learned that the mandates of an 1823 slavery "amelioration program," which required planters to improve the rights and conditions of *all* enslaved people, were not being implemented, they organized a strike.[1]

Historian Thomas C. Holt explains that this revolt, "in both rhetoric and tactics," was "a defensive war, intended to maintain rights, privileges, and territory" that the slaves thought had already been won. The rebellion thus began as a relatively nonviolent protest, in that only residences and trash storage buildings were targeted. Growing canes and human beings were not to be harmed, as both would be needed afterward, in the rebels' plot, at harvest time. But when the planters and the army drew up arms against them, the rebels fought back; by the end of their failed effort, in January, the rebels had inflicted more than 1 million pounds' sterling worth of property damage over 750 square miles in western Jamaica and suffered the loss of 540 of their own men—200 in combat, and the rest at the hands of firing squads and gallows.[2]

Although the British had quickly quelled the 1831 rebellion, and although the white colonial militia lost only fourteen lives, a spirit of rebellion had been awakened in Jamaica that could not be subdued. This time, however, it was the white planters' turn for retaliation; because the slaves' uprising had been led by members of the Baptist church, these planters began to attack Baptist and Methodist missionaries and churches—actions that lost them the sympathy of whites in Britain and that garnered support abroad for the growing abolitionist movement. The rebellion and its aftermath thus served the broader purpose of advancing the rights of slave laborers, as discussions of *gradual* abolition in the House of Commons soon shifted, by the fall of 1832, into discussions about "the necessity of *immediate* abolition." When the Abolition Act was passed on August 20, 1833, the authors cited the Christmas revolt of Jamaica "as a major factor compelling their action."[3]

In order to frame the importance of the event within the specific parameters of my discussion about transatlantic personhood—a practice constituted by movement, variation, and resistance—it is important to understand exactly *who* these slave rebels were and what was unique about their particular organization. I will thus begin my analysis with these New World Americans, whose hybrid cultural performance played a crucial role in the organization and advancement of their cause. I will use their example to highlight the broader historical shifts in the definition and performance of *culture* itself throughout the century, moving northward through the Atlantic, from Jamaica to the Arctic and back again, through the ethnographic gaze, travels, and writings of Franz Boas, Zora Neale Hurston, and Claude McKay. It is in the culminations of these travels and investments that my project will situate itself, for its remainder, in the twentieth century, albeit still bound to its fundamental questions about the role of transatlantic science and (un)disciplinarity in emerging assertions of personhood in the New World.

The rebels who led the Christmas Revolt of 1831, like many slave rebels who came before and after, expressed a true desire to cultivate the land as their own, as opposed to the chase of a grand but simplistically utopian ideal of freedom without further claims to labor or property rights. But they were emboldened to make these demands, in part, because they also represented a generational and societal shift in colonial society that rippled beyond the system of slavery but that certainly hastened its demise. The 1831 rebels were primarily Jamaican-born, literate, and well assimilated into colonial culture. In fact, many of them were considered to be part of their masters' inner circles—the plantation "elites," as mentioned earlier—who worked as drivers and artisans, and who capitalized on their relative mobility throughout the colony to both contemplate and organize.

But to fully understand the complexity of their organization, we must first unpack the power of their position as *Jamaican-born*. The slave rebels, as native-born Jamaicans of African descent, now also had a further link to their European cousins born in Jamaica, who shared the same birthplace but who had different rights based purely on the accident of (legitimized) descent. These rebels also possessed an organic, native claim to the land of their birth that they had toiled to harvest, and carried with them the inspiring example of (and refugees from) a victorious rebellion by their neighbors to the north against the Mother Country. These simultaneous claims of belonging to both the homeland and the metropole helped to fuel the rebels' fight and to confirm their cause as both legitimate and laudable. By working, in part, to both merge and overturn a historical narrative of "creolization" that prioritized *jus sanguinis* (the right of blood) over *jus soli* (territorial rights), the Jamaican rebels invite a more careful consideration of the work of intercultural performance and creolization to inaugurate political change.[4]

Although this chapter relies on a perhaps too-familiar lens of New World acts of creole cultural performance, my aim is to extricate and reanimate these fraught terms ("culture" and "creolization") from their current critical perception as insufficient, static, and vapid signifiers that depend too much on a celebratory, postimperial vision of the New World as the primary site of "hybridity" and "mixture." What I offer instead is a fresh look—albeit, through familiar geographical sites and figures—at the rise of ethnography as a *political* field that is foundationally and strategically linked to broader global histories and struggles of productive *undoings* as it is to narratives of postcolonial remaking.

I open with the Jamaican rebels' revolt in order to parallel it with later acts of "creolized cultural performance," labeling it thus not because it was a "hybrid" mixture of African, European, and American forces, nor because its New World location marks it as a singular or originary event. Rather, I contend that it rehearses a particular kind of political mimicry—a significant political intervention made possible through cultural performance that was not simply analogous to, but a foundational mirror for, twentieth-century ethnographers and artists like Franz Boas, Zora Neale Hurston, and Claude McKay. These practitioners and observers straddled, like their revolutionary predecessors across the Atlantic world (from spaces like Jamaica and Haiti to Sierra Leone, Liberia, Ethiopia, and elsewhere), multiple allegiances, affiliations, and performances. Such acts of Bhabhian mimicry, I argue, in which the Anglicized rebels use their understanding of and proximity to colonial power as disruptive strategy, offer a more nuanced, more political, and less static vision of "the culture concept," and perhaps even of "creolization."[5] Contentious and insufficient as these terms remain as we struggle to reconcile historical processes with academic theories about cross-cultural, cross-disciplinary contact and change in the Atlantic world, their shifting and varied meanings, their instability as placeholders, are vital to understanding the disruptive potential of transatlantic personhood in this era and thus invite our continued grappling.

Prior to Kamau Brathwaite's seminal work *The Development of Creole Society in Jamaica*, scholars had often studied this tiny commonwealth and surrounding regions most closely or often only in terms of slave society.[6] But Brathwaite's vision and the increasingly expansive views of those scholars who have followed are, like Jamaica itself, far more complicated, engaging a range of different groups whose bloodlines and birthrights had long been intertwined with one another. This creolization, as Brathwaite and others since have defined, critiqued, and honed it, was fundamental to the formation and politicization not just of Jamaica but also, of course, Africa, Europe, and other regions and groups that participated in the economic and political construction of larger, bounded yet intertwined Atlantic world cultures. Thus a full understanding of Jamaican society and its wider influence on the Atlantic world comes not simply from the organizational mechanism of slavery that brought Europeans and Africans together here, but of the relationships, affiliations, allegiances, and practices that came together in this space and that continued to prosper or shift in other spaces. Creolization, then, both preceded and exceeded any social or national designation of the region as *Jamaica* or even as part of "The New World."[7]

We should be careful in our readings of Atlantic spaces like Jamaica, cautions anthropologist Deborah Thomas, to avoid attributing a "folk" blackness to Jamaica's African heritage that would relegate it to the past or posit it as "a utopian vision of what blackness could do, could be, if it were to get with the creole program."[8] Instead, she advises scholars to read "modern blackness" in Jamaica with care and attention to local identities and relations of power that are often subsumed or erased under an essentializing creole nationalism.[9]

The term *creole*, derived from the Spanish *criollo*, meaning "one native to the settlement though not ancestrally indigenous to it," has had different cultural meanings in different geographic regions throughout history. In Brazil—as alluded to in chapter 2—it was a term reserved for locally born slaves of African descent. In late-nineteenth-century New Orleans and beyond, it increasingly applied only to "mulattoes," whereas in Louisiana more broadly, it was generally used to describe the white Francophone population. In the period leading to the Christmas Revolt of 1831, the term *creole* in Jamaica was used—in the traditional Spanish sense—to refer to *both* whites and slaves who were native to the colony, but who placed their ancestral origins elsewhere. The added overtone here, as in other colonies, Brathwaite explains, was one of authenticity and cultural autonomy.[10]

However, it is important to note that groups such as maroons—who did not interact, for obvious reasons, with those of European origin—were not part of the creole society. For, in Brathwaite's formulation, a key component of creolization is the balance between the "colonial arrangement" with a European power on one hand, and "a plantation arrangement" on the other. This heterogeneity is an essential element of creolization.[11]

Sidney Mintz and Richard Price add to this understanding of creole practice the commonplace ritual experimentation and mutual borrowing in West and Central Africa of religious practices, too, which "were relatively permeable to foreign influences and tended to be 'additive' rather than 'exclusive' in their orientation toward other cultures."[12] This permeability reveals that such fluctuating designations and ritual crossings were at play before the West defined "criollo." "We believe," explain Mintz and Price, "that the development of these social bonds, even before the Africans set foot in the New World, already announced the birth of new societies based on new kinds of principles."[13]

I have lingered over these shifts and definitions here in order to introduce the importance of a particular kind of creolization to the Christmas revolt, and in turn, the ways it modeled the political work of permeable cultural alliances, led as it was by rebels who were not only participating in a "colonial arrangement" with their European cousins but for whom the integration of Western and non-Western religious and cultural practices was a key factor in the organization and execution of the revolt. Led by black leaders of the Baptist Church, many have referred to the rebellion as the Baptist War, or, in more specific terms that I will detail below, the *Native* Baptist War. It was, thus, in many ways, too, a *Creole* Baptist war, made possible through the integration—even if temporary and under a false pretense of trust—of black and white native-born Jamaican persons, routed through Africa and Europe.

The rebel leaders of this Creole Christmas Revolt were not just congregants of the Baptist Church, but leaders and deacons. Using the trust and authority bestowed upon them by plantation foremen as a result of their church positions, leaders like Sam Sharpe worked to build up their own private church meetings outside the purview of British missionaries, "including separate services and an independent organizational network."[14]

These deacons-turned-rebels were members of an independent sect of the Baptist faith referred to as *Native* Baptists, a creolized version of the Baptist religion that mixed Christian traditions with traditional African religious practices. This religious hybridization can be traced to the previous generation of baptized slaves and freedmen who found refuge in Jamaica following the end of the American Revolution. It was under their influence, above that of white missionaries, explains Brathwaite, that "the *public* leadership of a large mass of slaves shifted from obeah-men to black preachers." This, of course, is a strong example of how a particular kind of creolization worked within Jamaican society, as two religious traditions merged to form a third religion.[15]

It was this version of Baptist practice, incorporating several African-Atlantic traditions, that not only helped Sam Sharpe and his fellow deacons and followers organize and plan this nonviolent strike-turned-rebellion but that also helped both sides realize, as the slogan of the rebellion reminded rebels and planters alike, that "no man can serve two masters."[16] Thus the act of interculturation, in this case, also served as an act of reclamation: a faith that, despite differences in cultural practice, belonged equally to both Africans and Americans, making equal demands of faith and humility on each.

What we (as perhaps did the rebels and planters) learn from an examination of this particular act of rebellion is something beyond even the human sacrifices made for the lofty ideals of freedom and salvation, and beyond a useful lesson in the early history of postcolonial Jamaica. What we learn is far more practical and applicable to the survival of cultures as a whole; for the malleability of cultural traditions and politicized creole performance teach us that the power of interculturation is one that—as Brathwaite and others have suggested—precedes, makes possible, and, as I will argue in the final chapter, has the power to destabilize the rhetoric of nationalism, imperial logic, and legally mandated or geographically rooted definitions and conceptions of personhood.

To relate Brathwaite's characterization to the broader scientific terms already laid out in my own discussion, we return to Darwin's implicit argument that to truly understand the function of evolution, we must stop prioritizing a human-centered approach to evolutionary change. We must, instead, understand that variation in nature preceded any organization or designation of the animal *human*. We can understand ourselves fully only in relation to the larger nature from which we emerge and are emerging still. New World regions (like Jamaica, and the other parts of the Americas visited by the *Beagle*), similarly, had to be considered not as mere by-products of slavery and colonization but as processual forces and shifting landscapes in their own right, resisting, accommodating, and ever-becoming societies. Creolization is not just a useful cultural parallel to Darwinian science but was also fundamental to Darwin's understanding of how evolution and adaptation occurs; for Darwin, too, saw Old and New World alliances in both nature and culture similar to those Brathwaite points to in his study of creole society.

Understanding creolization is thus key, as is evolutionary science, in helping us to see how ideas of the human were being reconfigured during the period of this study. Just as the merging of cultural forms and practices revealed the power of transatlantic personhood as a category-shifting and cultural-blending performance, so the introduction of an evolutionary model of human development—despite its mistranslations into a vision of Western progress and superiority—actually mirrored the instability of disciplinary categories.

One of the primary concerns of this chapter is the examination and interrogation of *culture* as both a shifting practice and an object of scientific study itself in the long nineteenth century, particularly in the Americas. If taxonomies of race, nation, and even subjectivity can be thought of as rhetorical placeholders for a process of constant becoming (and unbecoming), where does this leave the important yet often delimiting idea of culture, and the attempts to *capture* it as a field of study? Who would be best qualified to conduct the most authentic and unbiased study of it—a native inhabitant or the native returned? A transplanted immigrant or an outside observer?

Cultural practice as we have come to know it, especially in the New World, represents a kind of middle ground between accident and intent, and the story of its own transcontinental journey defies any logic of organically inscribed unity. But the evolution of the "culture concept" in the early twentieth century, like "creolization," has its own controversial genealogy and journey as a term that shifted from its position as an "anti-concept" that stood for "everything that race was not" (that is, if the logic of race was deterministic, biological, and fixed, then the logic of culture represented its opposite, as fluid, shifting, and routed through social and environmental ties) to a term that became, by midcentury, a synonymous substitute for race itself.[17] An "intellectual response to a political situation," as anthropologists like Jemima Pierre and others have explained, the "deployment of culture ironically reconciled the Boasian agenda with the taxonomic schemes of earlier times."[18] Thus in the name of relativism, ethnographers, sometimes unwittingly, marginalized and taxonomized groups further by treating communities "as cultural isolates."[19]

Contemporary scholars of culture thus implore us, in a similar refrain to Caribbeanist scholars who critique the limits of "creolization," to think about the *work* of ethnogenesis and group organization from a different angle. Brad Evans, for example, argues that the critical impulse to move "beyond culture" is yet another shift in terms that continues to "misunderstand the historical and systemic nature by which people share a sense of things." Instead, he asks readers to look back "before cultures" and examine more closely "what was already there, both 'before' and 'during' the period of culture's sway."[20]

Culture in its pre-Boasian formulation became most productively problematic when examined through the taxonomizing lens of science, which sought to differentiate and situate groups for its own ends—sometimes for noble if self-congratulatory attempts at preservation or documentation, or for more overtly suspicious aims of racial ranking or the determination of its potential for conversion, occupation, or eradication. Thus "Creole" culture (even in all its own variations) became distinct from maroon culture, which was, in turn, distinct from British Anglo-Saxon culture. This is not to refute *real* differences in cultural practice and organization within these groups, but it is the overall argument of this work that *all* encounters rehearse an inevitable permeability (even those that refuse or resist it) that is essential to understanding the operational logic of culture as a shifting concept that is always transforming and transformative. Thus even deliberate acts of self-imposed sequestration or segregation, useful as they are in helping us understand the *manufactured* nature of social relations, are less helpful in studying how culture, broadly constitutive of change and the unraveling of categories, actually works.

While I agree with the premise of scholars like Michael Elliott and Brad Evans that the process of performing, if not defining, *culture* in relativistic terms began long before Franz Boas legitimated the term as part of twentieth-century ethnographic discourse (as the Creole Baptists themselves exemplify), the evolution and bifurcation of its meaning in the post-Darwinian moment is of marked importance.[21] As Robert Young has suggested, the fact that Boas was able to transform the idea of "culture," once synonymous with "civilization," into "a relatively neutral word that described holistically the way of life of non-European societies . . . marks the moment when the doctrine of polygenism had finally declined out of view, lifting the racist penumbra that had overshadowed any consideration of cultures as distinct."[22] In other words, twentieth-century ethnographers like Boas and his student Zora Neale Hurston extricated "culture" from its long-synonymous association with "civilization" as a measure of human progress and achievement, associating the latter instead with the project of imperialism and defining the former as its societal antithesis.

Of course, Young is also clear in his definition that culture still functioned hierarchically within the frame of civilization in this period, especially with Europeans' emerging modernist interest in primitivism. In other words, explains Young, "at this point the hierarchy of higher and lower cultures within the scale of civilization around the world was transferred to European culture itself (with high culture paradoxically allying itself to non-European primitivism)." Culture, according to Young, was thus a bifurcated term that still embodied the implicit notion of "high" and "low" that had once been gathered under the umbrella of "civilization."[23]

The bifurcation that I would like to offer is contiguous with these critical perspectives but places its emphasis on a different pulse point of the culture concept: that is, that culture as performance deliberately resists culture as definite category. New World ethnographers and artists struggled in particularly difficult ways with this inevitable bifurcation as they straddled competing cultural desires in their own immigrant or creolized bodies and rehearsed the impossibility of authentic cultural representation, even as they demanded and depended upon the authenticity of their cultural investigations. So just as culture itself operated within and against Western civilization, so ethnography, too, participated in this same antithetical and "conflictual economy," miming alongside ever-shifting cultures themselves, "the tension between sameness and difference . . . cohesion and dispersion, containment and subversion."[24]

Transatlantic science played a significant role in shaping ethnographic study for the century ahead, not only through its own documentation and articulation of the creolizing effects of cultural experience and encounter but in the ways that it, too, negotiated competing visions of culture as an "accidental accretion of elements" on one hand and as an "integrated spiritual totality" on the other.[25] Franz Boas also points to common pitfalls between biological and anthropological models of inquiry, using Darwin's revolutionary scientific model—and its common mistranslation—as a cautionary tale for anthropologists. Lauding the impact of Darwin's influence on the natural sciences, Boas warns against the "irresistible" urge to look at the natural sciences from the viewpoint of Western history. "From the very beginning," he admonishes, "there has been a strong tendency to combine with the historical aspect a subjective valuation of the various phases of development. . . . The oft-observed change from simple forms to more complex forms, from uniformity to diversity, was interpreted as a change from the less valuable to the more valuable, and thus the historical view assumed in many cases an ill-concealed teleological tinge." It is this basic mistranslation that still plagues anthropological and natural sciences, Boas insists, obscuring the otherwise "grand picture of nature" (or culture, as Boas would later formalize) offered by Darwin as "a unit of ever-changing form and color, each momentary aspect being determined by the past moment and determining the coming changes."[26]

Boas's enormous influence on twentieth-century anthropology makes him a foundational presence in the work of the transatlantic figures that populate the rest of this study, not only through his work in the North Atlantic region of Baffin Island but also, and perhaps most significantly, through the work of his students and colleagues like Zora Neale Hurston (whose work in Jamaica, alongside that of her contemporary Claude McKay, is highlighted at the end of this chapter), Katherine Dunham, and Melville Herskovits (whose experiences and research in Haiti are discussed in chapter 4). In addition to the mark of his legacy on their projects and mine, any discussion of the shifting position of culture(s) on the brink of the twentieth century would be lean at best without an analysis of Boas's own inspirations and struggles to define, respect, capture, and represent indigenous groups, all the while grappling with the promise and peril introduced by European scientific and social intervention, and of his own vexed role within that larger project.

Franz Boas conducted his early research on Baffin Island, in the Arctic, in 1883, after which he went to work at the Royal Ethnological Museum in Berlin, where artifacts were exhibited according to a geographic model that he would later advocate and implement in American museums. At the time of his immigration to the United States in 1887, American anthropology was still based on an evolutionary model of development, which did not provide any context about geographical or tribal specificity.[27] Displeased by the application of biological categories such as "species, genus, and family" onto the realm of human behavior, Boas proposed instead "a detailed study of customs in their relation to the total culture of the tribe practicing them, in connection with an investigation of their geographical distribution."[28] His increasing professional emphasis on tribal specificity and acculturation was also influenced by his own personal experience as a perpetual outsider throughout his life; as a Jew in Germany and as a German-Jewish immigrant to the United States, Boas understood quite personally and asserted rather troublingly that adaptation and accretion were vital to cultural organization, change, and survival. As anthropologist Leonard Glick has discussed, Boas struggled throughout his life to reconcile these "two linked but conflicting elements in his personal history," a tension that undoubtedly informed his work in cultural relativism, even if highlighting the irony of it. For even as Boas supported the need for cultural pride and the maintenance of some ethnic heritage ties for groups like African Americans, American Indians, and even German Americans, he also "advocated assimilation to the point of literal disappearance for Jews."[29]

Although Boas built a career in ethnography that worked to unmoor the notion of "Volk"—a term used by Germans to demarcate their own exclusive ethnicity—from its strict, genetically determined, nativist interpretation, he nevertheless could not grant *himself* access to that term without shedding his own religious heritage.[30] Volkish ideology and anti-Semitism were pervasive features of German life during Boas's university years (1877–81), explains Glick, sentiments "that no Jewish student could ignore."[31] But as German Jews fled to the United States for safe harbor, they often found they faced continued hostility, not only from non-Jewish Americans but from more established German-Jewish immigrants, who were determined to abandon their Jewish identities in order to assimilate, a policy of adaptation that Boas would soon come to advocate.[32]

Yet in his study of the dissemination of folktales, for example, Boas hints that culture—through his explication of these myths and their distribution—is a mixture of the organic and the foreign, as tales are adapted through the ever-changing *volksgeist* (genius of the people).[33] Interculturation and intervention were an inevitable part of cultural growth and development, as Boas had himself struggled to learn (and unlearn, depending on the context) in a very personal, albeit conflicted, way, from both his own experiences in Germany and the United States as well as from his fieldwork among the Kwakiutl and Inuit in the 1880s and beyond.[34] Thus a vital question to consider in an examination of Boas's early fieldwork with the Inuit regards the extent to which Boas's choice to work with these *other* indigenous groups of the Americas—those in the Arctic, and not the descendants of the transatlantic slave trade—was fueled, in part, by a desire for influence that was not entirely innocent of an imperial, Volkish fantasy. As Julia E. Liss argues, "In organizing his expedition, Boas exploited contemporary interest in exploration and travel to faraway places." The second half of the nineteenth century, as we have already seen, brought together a host of nationalist, colonial, and scientific interests, encouraging European and American expeditions, especially to places with apparent exotic appeal, such as Africa, Asia, and the Arctic. "Bourgeois fascination with the 'primitive' and 'strange,'" explains Liss, fueled this desire, "enabling geographic societies, which took an active role in funding expeditions in Germany and England as well as America, to build large followings."[35] For Boas, the experience of fieldwork promised a kind of inoculation, as the fulfillment of his "fantasy of penetrating an alien society without causing disturbance" might help cure him of his own ontological exile: he would possess the knowledge of an insider yet treat his subjects with respect. A second, related question that frames this examination is the extent to which ethnographers like Boas, and the populations they come to study, can mutually influence each other's cultural affiliations, allegiances, and practices. For the Inuit, this accidental interculturation would come with grave consequences.[36]

Despite several years of intermittent contact with Europeans from the 1590s onward, much like the Fuegians before FitzRoy's experiment (and, to some extent, the Accompong maroons of Jamaica who are discussed later in this chapter), the Inuit of Baffin Island, north of Hudson Bay, had never lived alongside Europeans or been significantly influenced by non-native cultures. As Douglas Cole explains in an essay about Boas's Baffin Island letter-diaries from his early 1883 expedition, Boas's motivation to study the Inuit is not immediately apparent. Cole hypothesizes that "perhaps the choice was quite a personal one, its roots lying far back in Boas's youth. As early as 1870, when he was but a boy of twelve, he wrote to his sister of undertaking an expedition to the north or South Pole after completing university."[37] As he grew older, his Humboldtian passion for travel grew into a deeper investment in the role of environmental dependence on the Inuit way of life; his boyhood passion took professional hold when he enrolled in a course on the geography of polar regions in 1878–79 at Bonn. But his youthful inspiration is not to be discounted, as it reveals the complex negotiations between performance and authenticity that limn all investments in travel and encounter and reminds us that cultural (or imperial) fantasy and cultural practice were inextricably linked for all traveling scientists of this period.

These negotiations are quite apparent in Boas's earliest fieldwork, in the unposted love letters he wrote to his fiancée, Marie Krackowizer, which document his fifteen-month journey among the Inuit from 1883 to 1884. Boas's unposted correspondence, often written alongside journal entries, resulted in "a single, 500-page letter composed over a fifteen-month period," that is, in large part "an extended love letter, in which amorous effusions often overwhelm descriptions of his field activities."[38] There appears to be no real difference between his journal entries and the letters to Marie, except that the epistolary genre allows him to hail an implied (Western, female, leisure) reader. Through this seemingly simple act of interpellation, Boas is able to maintain a level of narrative distance from those he observes and to retain his own sense of cultural authority. He is always in a scientific, pedagogical pose, providing evidence that will help Marie (and others) to *visualize* his life with the Inuit, performing both the authenticity of his experience as well his expertise on his chosen subject(s).

At the start of his journey, Boas conjures Marie's image to evoke a sense of familiarity and calm amid the unfamiliar geography of Kikkerton, linking these two worlds through the parallel aesthetic beauty of his new, noble landscape, and the familiar face of his beloved. As he writes in a September 12, 1883, entry: "I had provided for my six Eskimo. I sat alone, the only person awake on the rocks, watching the ice. I had time and peace to think about my sweet love. The deep water was at my feet. Opposite me arose the steep and threatening black cliffs, the rapids we had crossed that afternoon rushed and roared at my side, and in the far distance shone the snow-covered mountain. But I saw only you, my Marie. You and the noble beauty of my surroundings made me conscious of the immensity of our separation."[39]

Boas's letters, as a genre, seem to reflect a Romantic tradition of nostalgia and rootedness more than an emerging ethnographic tradition of relativism. But in a sense, they allow him to straddle these two worlds, resulting in a document that highlights the impossibility of cultural purity or "featureless" observation, on either side. They are a necessary outlet, too, for they function as both the vehicle that keeps Boas grounded in Western reality, as well as the stage on which he can perform his cultural cross-dress.

Thus, his narrator is one who roams the region as a lone surveyor—*his* Eskimo asleep—dressed in the warm caribou fur provided by them, living among them as adopted kin and, perhaps, temporary king. Eventually, he purports to have succumbed to Inuit life, stating in a February 1884 journal entry: "I am now a true Eskimo. I live as they do, hunt with them, and belong to the men of Anarnitung. I have hardly any European food left, eat only seal and drink coffee."[40] Through his experiences, and through the act of narration, Boas indoctrinated, or authenticated, himself into Inuit culture.

Boas's varied poses throughout his letter-diaries, as ethnographer, writer, Inuit, doctor, lover—are performances that make his research and experiences *feel* more authentic to him, even as their grandiosity unveils the ruse of his *actual* immersion. However, the interjection of *others'* bodies, specifically through the entrance of disease among the Inuit, betrays the façade of Boas's controlled performance, providing proof of mutual contact and cultural penetration.

When diphtheria first breaks out in Kikkerton in the fall of 1883, the Inuit call upon Boas for assistance, as they believe he is a medical doctor. He does not correct their misconception, even as they invite him to sit at the bedside of children and adults who have suddenly become ill shortly after Boas and his party enter the village.

In a November 1883 entry, he writes: "This morning I sat in a tiny, tiny snow hut at the deathbed of a poor little Eskimo boy. The Eskimo are so confident that the Doctora'dluk, as they call me, can help them when they are sick, that I always go to them when they call me. And I am always unhappy when I am with those poor people that I cannot help them." Later on in the same entry, he announces, as if he has accepted his own role as doctor, "I have another patient, a woman with pneumonia."[41] It seems, from these entries, as though there is a strange ethnographic interculturation happening here, as Boas takes on the role of Inuit healer, even as it is his presence that is likely infecting the group.

Soon, however, the illnesses become a nuisance to Boas, as the competing reality of the Inuit community interrupts his professional goals and needs, as the illnesses literally cause a delay in Boas's cultural *costume*: On December 9, 1883, he writes from Kikkerton: "Unfortunately, there are again two children very sick with a diphtheria-like sickness, [and] both died. . . . This will cause an unpleasant disruption to the making of my caribou suit as the women will not work for three days."[42]

As the cases of diphtheria become more widespread, Boas refuses to acknowledge any potential complicity of his crew in the spread of the outbreak, instead blaming his banishment from the Inuit community on their own superstitious belief. Despite his attempt to hold on to a sense of respect for the cultural beliefs that he believes are at the root of his maltreatment, and despite the seeming air of condescension in Boas's narration, his perceptions are complicated by his sincere belief that he is an ousted *member* of the community.

While no one from Boas's party had suffered from diphtheria on their journey, their ships, the *Germania* and the *Catherine*, were the only ones to have sailed through the area at that time, so it is more than likely the disease traveled into the Inuit communities with them. The Inuit performed an incantation to unearth the cause of this fast-moving, fatal epidemic and came to the conclusion that Boas and his party were to blame. Although

Boas received word that the local population no longer wanted his presence among them, and although James S. Mutch—the Scottish manager of the Kikkerton whaling station at Cumberland Sound, who was fluent in Inuktitut and provided invaluable assistance to Boas as a translator and facilitator during his field study—decided (out of fear and respect for the reigning sentiment of distrust among the Inuit) to remain at the station, Boas persevered, arguing that "this kind of hostility should not be allowed to prevail."[43]

Again, Boas's continued insistence on visiting the Inuit, despite their growing protests, can be read as either the exertion of a Western interloper's perceived sense of racial dominance and entitlement or as a cultural insider's sense of inherent belonging. In either case, it is, in fact, a usurpation, as he relies on his knowledge of their strong cultural sense of hospitality and superstition to continue his visits to the communities from which he has been banished, knowing they will not dare to refuse him entry. In January 1884, he narrates his troubles with his former Inuit hosts, like Oxaitung and others, but decides to go on with his travels as planned, even as Mutch refuses to go with him:

> On Thursday somebody came from Anarnitung with the news that Oxaitung's wife was apparently worse, not better. He also reported that many Eskimo blamed me for it, as it really seems as though sickness and death follows my footsteps. If I were superstitious, I really would believe that my presence brought misfortune to the Eskimo! Many are supposed to have said that they did not wish to see me in their iglu again, nor Mutch. He became frightened because of this so I set out alone today, Monday, the twenty-first. Just as I expected, I was received here just as kindly as before and am now at home in Tininixdjuax.[44]

Confused and frustrated by his excommunication, yet quite accustomed to being read, in his own personal life, as an outsider, Boas continues to cross boundaries as he sees fit, setting his own rules about cultural penetration and viewing the Inuits' fear of him only in relation to his own troubles. A few weeks later, he writes from Nexemiarbing: "I have to suffer a great deal because of the sickness that is prevalent here. I know that many Eskimo are unwilling to deal with me although they do not dare show it openly. None of them wanted to lend me dogs, but when I asked them they did not dare refuse."[45]

The diphtheria incident highlights the ways in which ethnographers and scientists were complicit in hastening the inevitable process of interculturation and also points to some foundational post-Boasian eth-nographic dilemmas: How does the ethnographer reconcile the anxiety of his/her own influence on the population s/he studies? If this influence is an inevitable symptom of ethnographic research, then how is it ever pos-sible to create a *truly* authentic ethnographic narrative that is not imbued with fiction or bias, and that is not immediately outdated, as the culture one enters is never the same as the culture one exits? Finally, as Boas expe-rienced throughout his career, how does one negotiate one's own cultural position (as non-Inuit, as German, as Jewish, as American) in conducting and presenting ethnographic research? For his firm stance on the com-monalities of different races, Boas was publicly rebuked by eugenicists like Lothrop Stoddard who mocked him as "a pathetic Jew pitifully trying to pass as white."[46]

Franz Boas knew, on multiple levels, as did his student, Zora Neale Hurston, what it meant to be a cultural outsider and to have one's cultural *authenticity* depend on its translatability across multiple disciplines, cul-tures, and geographic terrains. This shared perspective gave both scholars a keen insight into the constitution of culture as malleable and shifting, not only because their survival had depended on it and not only because their hope for the future of cultural progress rested on it but because it gave them a power to manipulate their positions in it and their representa-tions of it.

Zora Neale Hurston began her work in the field of racial anthropology during a period of dramatic flux. From the 1920s to post–World War II, American anthropology shifted its angle of inquiry in questions of cul-tural determinism from a position of affirmation (a eugenicist model) to a position of challenge (a relativist, environmentalist model).[47] Hurston herself did much to challenge the deterministic, imperial logic of anthro-pology, but the foundation for her own ethnographic work was laid by the important strides made by her Columbia mentor, Franz Boas, who championed this new brand of anthropology. Boas paved the way for a new way of studying culture that countered the racist logic of a social Dar-winist model that imagined blacks as the "atavistic precursors to white civilization."[48]

However, it is important to note, as I have conveyed above, that the Boasian model of cultural relativity was not devoid of a certain subjective tone, language, and hermeneutic perspective that reflected and continued to fuel the pervasive racism of his era. As Aldona Jonaitis, director of the

University of Alaska Museum, discusses in a study on Boas and indigenous art, even his early work in salvage anthropology, which sought to
capture and preserve the "pure" precontact condition of American Indians by "recording the last remnants of an allegedly 'dying culture,'" fueled
a "nostalgia for the 'primitive' and the imperialist illusion of a 'vanishing
race.'"[49] In fact, as Karen Jacobs argues, Boas's very retention of the category of "the primitive" keeps his theory linked to the earlier racist model
of anthropology. The institutional origins of "the primitive" as a categori-
cal concept, notes Jacobs, "were arguably imbricated in the objectifying
gaze of anthropology's participant-observer practice and its structurally
implicit hierarchies as well."[50] Thus even though Boas works to divorce the
term from its racist connotation, he still retains the category as scientifically viable, thus confirming, in his 1911 *The Mind of the Primitive Man*,
that primitives simply cannot properly differentiate between human and
animal because they adhere to "idiosyncratic, irrational classification systems that arise from unconscious processes."[51]

This is where students like Hurston and her contemporaries in the Harlem Renaissance entered. Hurston comprehended, at an early point in her
career, the conflicted politics of the participant-observer method, and how
the hierarchies it sought to dismantle through its findings were the same
ones it relied upon to implement its studies and to retain its scientific status
of objectivity and authority. She did not have to travel to Jamaica and Haiti,
as she did later in her career, to learn this. She first performed, and perhaps first contemplated, the complexity of her position as budding African
American ethnographer when Boas asked her to conduct anthropometric
studies on the streets of Harlem in 1926, to walk around with a tape measure
in her hand, approaching black heads to appraise, record, and report back to
him.[52] Of course, the aim of Boas's study was to disprove biological racism
through this work, but the hierarchical structure that made this task a peculiar one for an African American woman could not have been lost on the
young Hurston, and it was undoubtedly not lost on Boas, either. Such early
autoethnographic projects set Hurston apart from other students trained in
the Boas school, and he and colleague Melville Herskovits eagerly encouraged Hurston to "capitalize on [the] duality" of her role as both "subject and
object of her discipline."[53] Hurston's position allowed her to collapse the
once-impassable distance between observer and observed, while still retain-
ing the necessary scientific objectivity of the discipline.

How could she possibly resist? Hurston took these problems of Boasian anthropology, imbued them with her own brand of study and

performance, and created a new way of looking at cultures, one that respected yet playfully distorted the perceptual and scientific logic of the participant-observer method. She employed techniques "that would embody African American expressive culture on its own terms, while also avoiding, as she told Langston Hughes, "loop-holes for the scientific crowd to rend and tear us."[54] Through a unique merging of anthropological discourse and African-Atlantic cultural practices, Hurston recast Boas's understanding of fieldwork as "a project of heroic alienation" and showed, instead, that "scientific objectivity is itself cultural."[55] Through this understanding, Hurston was able to navigate the unique position of ethnographer in cultural camouflage while keeping (mostly) intact her faith in the objectivity of ethnographic practice. She remained true to the fundamental principles of anthropological inquiry, combining objectivity and performance, merging reality with art.[56]

Hurston positioned herself early for this new exploration, stating in a March 29, 1927, letter to Boas: "The Negro is not living his lore to the extent of the Indian. . . . His Negroness is being rubbed off by close contact with the white world."[57] She thus employs the logic of salvage anthropology as part of her personal plea to be allowed an opportunity to make a more studied examination of Afro-Atlantic culture, while also, perhaps, making a subtle dig at Boas about the threat of her own cultural erasure as a professional pawn of white anthropology. Once she begins her work, Hurston finds that the cultures she explores are nowhere near extinction but have instead reappropriated the original violent gesture of white contact to create "dynamic, changing, lively 'hybrid' communities" that thrive both through and against their contact with other cultures.[58]

As she believed in the objectivity of her ethnographic work, Hurston did attempt, as she tells Boas in a letter about her work for *Mules and Men* (1935), "to be as exact as possible. Keep to the exact dialect as closely as I could, having the story teller to tell it to me word for word as I write . . . so that I shall not let myself creep in unconsciously."[59] One might read Hurston's letter playfully and argue that while she may have been exact in her transcriptions, and while she may have resisted letting her "self" creep in *unconsciously*, that she is no doubt, *consciously* very present—in a multi-layered way—in both her ethnographic work as well as her fiction, deliberately and fervently creating and disrupting authenticity *through* play, not as a means of providing a facile, uncomplicated, static, or false vision of black life for chauvinistic whites but, rather, one that is dynamic, shifting, slightly aloof, and unquantifiable by anyone's tape measure but her own.

Hurston brings together this chapter's opening concerns with creolization and the scientific problem of situating culture, with its closing
examination of ethnographic fiction as a resistant and nuanced response
against the yoke of authenticity, and a subtle undoing of static representa-
tions of personhood and culture. As an African American female artist-
ethnographer, Hurston understood the complicated nature of *captivity*
and *mobility* in the determination and study of diasporic communities
of African descent, and as such, she both employed and appreciated the
"feather-bed resistance" of diasporic peoples to those who came to study
them—a strategy of polite but firm evasion in which the probing interloper "is allowed to enter," as she explains, but is then "smothered under
a lot of laughter and pleasantries."[60] African Americans of the twentieth
century, themselves a creolized people, had long occupied a conflicted
stance to *American* culture, both resisting what Paul Gilroy has called
the "volkish popular cultural nationalism" yet asserting their rights and
privileges both within and (for some, before emancipation) beyond the
nation's legal parameters of personhood.[61]

But I contend that it was Hurston's arrival in Jamaica that awakened
in her a full realization of the complexity of her position, not just as an
African American, a woman, and an ethnographer, or even just the simultaneous weight of all these positions bearing on her at once; she had been
negotiating these dilemmas long before her Caribbean travels. Rather,
what Hurston learned—through the performance of her Afro-Atlantic
personhood in the Caribbean—was her power in this particular form of
professional exile, one that allowed her to move in and out of cultural
identifications, sometimes according to her own fluid performance and
sometimes according to the translations and readings of others. Hurston's
experiences in Jamaica and the writings provoked by her Caribbean journeys can thus be read, within the context of this chapter's larger focus, as a
professional, twentieth-century reenactment of the nomadic personhood
performed by the Creole Baptists of 1831 and their own acts of cultural
reconstruction and resistance a century earlier.[62]

By the time Hurston left for Jamaica and Haiti in 1936, she had moved
away from Boas's strict scientific method and had begun exploring the
rich history of folklore and the black vernacular alongside other young
artists of the Harlem Renaissance. Conducting her research on a Guggen-
heim fellowship, Hurston was further unfettered from the controlling arm
of her patron, Mrs. Charlotte Osgood Mason, who wielded much power
over Hurston and the other Harlem Renaissance artists she supported.[63]

Hurston's research methodology and its culminating product—a book-length study of African religious and cultural traditions in Jamaica and Haiti—represented an act of cultural and artistic hybridity: part ethnography, part fiction; part "authentic" folklore.

Hurston understood that her dual role as objective scientist and cultural insider brought both opportunity and struggle. She addresses this in her simultaneously subtle and deliberate style in the introduction to her 1935 *Mules and Men*. She begins by addressing the general difficulty of collecting information, explaining, "the best source is where there are the least outside influences and these people, usually under-privileged, are the shyest." She then moves on to the particular difficulty of collecting information from the African American, stating, "the Negro, in spite of his open-faced laughter, his seeming acquiescence, is particularly evasive." From here, Hurston makes a sudden pronoun shift that transports her from behind the camera lens to the photo itself, as she shifts from ethnographer to subject, suddenly teaching readers not about *these* people but about *we* people. "You see," she begins, "*we* are a polite people and we do not say to our questioner, 'Get out of here!' We smile and tell *him* something that satisfies the white person because, knowing so little about *us*, *he* doesn't know what *he* is missing."[64]

Hurston thus signals her position as both an outside observer of black culture and as an insider within it, collapsing the distance between observer and observed, and extricating the anthropological gaze from the fetishistic fantasy of the imperial, touristic reader who wants simply to "go native." Hurston's self-disclosure removes the possibility of such an experience for the white reader, in particular, pronouncing, from the start of her study, her unique narrative power and the double distance it creates for the twice-removed watcher of the complex drama about to unfold.

Just over a century after the Native Baptist war, Hurston's study of Jamaica demonstrates the continued power of shifting alliances in Atlantic spaces. While critics have denigrated her 1938 *Tell My Horse* as reactionary and blindly patriotic, especially for its performance of support for the American occupation of Haiti, I would like to suggest that its power and its nuance lie not in its nationalist or imperialist rhetoric (which in itself could be debated as a necessarily ironic performance) but in its revelation of *culture* and *personhood* as costumes that can and must be changed or shed, depending on region, status, or situation.[65] This is not to suggest that a creolized vision of culture or persons is a utopian solution to those bound to and limited by these categories. But what Hurston shows in *Tell My Horse*, despite its critical reception, is the power of this twoness that allows the border-crosser to extricate cultural practice from national interests, as needed, and then suture them as needed, too; this tension between resistance and accommodation is one that Hurston certainly employs in her research and personal life and that she finds mirrored, as a constitutional element of culture, in both Haiti and Jamaica.

Hurston, ever navigating the space between cultural outsider (as an African American and as an artist-ethnographer conducting research) and cultural insider (as one bound by a shared legacy of Atlantic migration and creolization), creates a persona in her narration that alternates between them. The narrator opens with a clear expertise about the region that she wishes to share with first-time armchair travelers, hinting, in the first lines of the study that "Jamaica . . . has something else besides its mountains of majesty and its quick, green valleys."[66] But she quickly moves from critical expert to fellow neophyte, allying herself with her presumably U.S. audience as she explains that "the island has its craze among the peasants known as Pocomania. . . . It is important to a great number of people in Jamaica, so perhaps we ought to peep in on it a while."[67]

Shifting constantly between that of expert and interloper, empathetic participant and incredulous witness, Hurston's narration mirrors the hybridity of the culture she has entered. This is evident in the first religious ritual of "pocomania" she describes, a creolized practice that incorporates African obeah practices and Christian rituals and retellings, all "enlivened by very beautiful singing." Hurston uses this soft landing into Jamaican creolization as an introduction to the larger "social viewpoints and stratifications which influence so seriously its economic direction." But even here, Hurston's narration plays with identification, comparing some Jamaicans' desire to imitate the British with some Americans' insistence on "aping the English as best they can even though they had one hundred and fifty years in which to recover."[68] By making a nationalist parallel instead of a racial one (even though she has already spelled out the demographics of Jamaica as a colony which is only 2 percent white, and 98 percent mixed with those of African descent), Hurston makes a direct link between Jamaica's troubles with social stratification and those of the United States. Thus she confronts her U.S. readers early with their own creolization. Since the United States forged its own independence from the same colonial master and is populated by descendants of other lands, its postrevolutionary identity crisis serves as a powerful parallel to the struggles of its Jamaican brethren.

Rich with folktales and parables that highlight the importance of *incorporating*—often literally—New and Old World traditions as rites of passage, Hurston arguably strikes both a pedagogical and contemplative pose, grappling with the significance of her own diasporic identification with the practices she has come to study. One such story begins after Hurston's narrator has engaged in a heated debate with a Jamaican man about love. He tells her of his firm belief that neither men nor women of the Occident have a proper understanding of "the function of love in the scheme of life."[69] This is followed by his promise to show her how "specialists" in Jamaica prepare young girls for love. Curious to learn, despite her anger at the man's reductive statements about *her* women and their overly intellectual ambitions, Hurston then observes and conveys to her readers the specifics of this prenuptial ritual.

These specialists—older women who are either widowed or otherwise "removed from active service"—are reinducted into the society on this advisory level. The goal of these specialists—and the society at large—is "to bring complete innocence and complete competence together in the same girl." After several days of being untouched, but simply lectured on how she must *position* herself for her husband for the proper consummation of marriage, she is then given—on her wedding day—a sensual massage by one of these specialists, receiving a "light-fingered manipulation down the body" until she swoons. She is then revived by "a mere sip of rum in which a single leaf of ganga has been steeped." The ritual is repeated several times until the girl is finally "in a twilight state of awareness, cushioned on a cloud of love thoughts." She thus walks down the aisle "with the assurance of infinity . . . and such eagerness in her as she went!"[70]

Though this ritual can be read (deliberately) as overly traditional in its advocacy of sexual acquiescence as the primary function of wives and as "primitive" in its emphasis on female arousal (and initiated as a woman-on-woman act), the subtlety of Hurston's metaphor is worth dissecting. There is something profound about a ritual that capitalizes on stereotypes of both the overly modern woman (as symptomatic of the disease of the Western world) *and* the so-called primitivism of African-inspired traditions. But Hurston undoes these stereotypes in a subtle and unexpected manner: For though the act of love is narrated, via lecture, in decidedly *colonial* terms (of the husband as master, and the act of love as a female labor that requires complete submission), it is demonstrated in a ritual that highlights and emphasizes female pleasure and is introduced and performed first by a woman on a woman. Thus despite the *official* purpose of the initiation rite, its actual lesson is not about penetration, labor, and conquest but, rather, about the importance of self-possession (or more specifically, other-possession) as linked not to patriarchy but to female community, introducing the young girl to the power of her own bodily possibilities.

One might read this parable, also, as a rewriting of what Laura Doyle has referred to as the "swoon" moment—the "phoenix fall" that often accompanies, in English-language novels, "the trope of an Atlantic crossing": from Olaudah Equiano's fainting on the ship that would transport him into slavery, to Reuel Briggs's fainting and subsequent revival into African kingship in Hopkins's *Of One Blood*. Although the young girl in Hurston's tale is not *literally* crossing Atlantic waters, the metaphor of the Atlantic crossing is certainly implied in the ritual's goal of transforming innocence into experience and preparing her for the service function of her new institution. For Doyle, the swoon moment involved "a bodily 'undoing' or 'ruin' that is often sexual or coded as feminine." In this moment, the old social identity is lost, and the self reawakens to find itself "uprooted and yet newly racialized." It is an association that is tied, for African-Atlantic writers, to the experience of the Middle Passage and, within an even older discursive frame, to "the classical set of associations between rape and the founding of republics."[71]

Hurston reverses this swoon moment, turning the moment of bodily undoing into a moment of communal reentry. This is, to be sure, not without its own costs—the girl, after all, is not freed from institutional conscription. But she awakens with a new and powerful understanding of the difference between rhetoric and experience. Like Hurston, she learns that rhetorical categories like *love* and *wife*, *culture* and *person*, are just that—contextual terms that are continually remade and reconfigured, through varied life experiences and in the crossing of permeable borders—geographic, sexual, ontological.

Through her travels and her folktales, Hurston thus resituates the African Atlantic narrative of displacement as a rehearsal or reenactment of cultural fluidity. In other words, through these unstable navigations between self-possession or self-assertion and communal accountability Hurston's subjects neither succumb to an alienated sense of double consciousness, nor do they espouse a naïve belief in a coherent, unified black folk culture. Rather, they construct their personhood in the space in between.

In addition to the ethnographic fables and folk traditions of Jamaica and Haiti that she compiled for *Tell My Horse*, Hurston also wrote her most acclaimed piece of fiction during her time in the Caribbean. *Their Eyes Were Watching God* was written in 1937, while she was completing her fieldwork in Haiti. Although the novel takes place in the United States, it is imbued with Hurston's transcultural, transdisciplinary experiences in the Caribbean, rich with actors and watchers with noses pressed against the glass; amateur ethnographers in folk camouflage sit on porches and assemble in courtrooms, staring, listening, and, in part, directing the drama they have come to witness and record. Janie Crawford, the principal character—evocative of that young Jamaican bride from *Tell My Horse* who is initiated into a performative understanding of diasporic culture and creolized, communal personhood—moves undaunted, staring provocatively into the camera and inviting readers into her world, linking ethnographic vision with its inevitable traits of performance and collusion.

The opening of the novel alludes to something that I have tried to address in my readings above but that is never openly reconciled in the ethnographic renderings of either Hurston or Boas—and that is, the position of ethnographers, both personally and professionally, as watchers in exile, always *between* cultures. Were their assertions of professional mobility in part aimed at resolving their feelings of personal exile? Do their stagings provide a broader pedagogical lesson about the position of outsiderliness as the only possible ontology for the anthropologist, or for the transcultural person?

"Ships at a distance have every man's wish on board," begins the narrator of *Their Eyes*, putting readers in the position of free, shorebound spectators who see in those structures not the trauma of the unilateral journey into captivity but, rather (and perhaps naïvely), the possibilities for mobility, capital, the dream of an *elsewhere*. The narrator continues, now inserting a gendered caveat to this vision that shifts its interpretation, and that guides the rest of the narrative:

> For some they come in with the tide. For others they sail forever on the horizon, never out of sight, never landing until the Watcher turns his eyes away in resignation, his dreams mocked to death by Time. That is the life of men. Now, women forget all those things they don't want to remember, and remember everything they don't want to forget. The dream is the truth. Then they act and do things accordingly.[72]

It is women, in Hurston's vision here, who are able to turn away from the false, colonial, patriarchal promise of the ship on the horizon, not with resignation and regret but with a practical strategy aimed at future survival, turning to the legacy of mobility and transculturation carried in their *own* memories, bodies, and histories, reclaiming and reinventing the terms of their outsiderliness on their own shores. Rather than chasing the mirage of a false frontier, they will build on the work they have begun together, in their postcolony here at home. Transculturation, then, shifts from a logic of imposition, conquest, and naïve fantasy to a logic of introspection, self-carriage, and remaking. This vision is one, I would argue, eventually realized by Boas and Hurston, who, through their own *acts* of journeying, learn to reinvent themselves, not through a resolution of their exiled status but through its professional embrace.

Of course, this embrace is not without its tensions and misgivings for either Boas or Hurston. But these were not just parallel idiosyncrasies common to both teacher and student. They were symptomatic of the larger cultural and scientific struggles with creolization and the navigation of personhood with which many Atlantic travelers and writers grappled in the twentieth century. Anthropology as a discipline could not universalize transcultural experience (nor should it) but worked, instead, to legitimize the subversive and creative possibilities of fragmentation and destabilization. Although these possibilities had already been rehearsed in the Atlantic world through subversive acts of cultural formation, contact, and resistance for centuries, it took the growth of anthropology as a discipline to model how transatlantic cultures emerged (and were emerging still) from them.

In fact, as mentioned earlier, scholars like Julia Liss, Brad Evans, and others have argued that an overemphasis on "the culture concept" as "the paradigmatic development in the history of anthropology" has led to the neglect of its primary concerns with "transience" and "interrelationships."[73] While Boas, and perhaps even Hurston, set out with a scientifically rooted desire to *capture* and document cultures untouched by the "modern," what their findings and encounters reveal are continuous overlaps—whether freshly imposed or long-embedded, whether inter- or intracultural—between West and non-West, Christian and Obeah, outsiders and insiders, bound by a creolization that mirrored these ethnographers' own narratives of self-discovery and change, both before and through their professional fieldwork. Complicit itself in the erasure of the fiction of cultural singularity, this new strand of twentieth-century anthropology recognized that the foundation of cultural difference was located *not* in the bodies or geographies of individuals but in the act of encounter itself. Its practitioners thus manipulated the power of encounter to challenge and undo this fiction of stasis and uniquity—demonstrating a creolization that is by no means simple or utopian or celebratory in every case, or always a merging of "Old" and "New" worlds, but is always and necessarily a political act of remaking.

As this work makes its way through the twentieth century, I would like to offer more backward glances to those ships on the shoreline of decades past, and those figures that remind us of how we arrived here, and how we have come to carry the conflicted legacies of those circum-navigations— those of imperial and economic conquest, those of scientific discovery, and those of personal and political devastation—inside our own bodies, and through our conjoined histories, geographies, and narratives. For just as the influence of Darwin's early encounters and observations are reflected in the work and encounters of twentieth-century ethnographers like Franz Boas and Zora Neale Hurston, so, in turn, is this layered impact of encounter and the development of ethnographic vision reflected in African-Atlantic literary responses against the essentializing primitivism of the Harlem Renaissance.

The fiction of Claude McKay moves through this "both/and" space, since this struggle was reflected in his own history as a Jamaican national who negotiated his hyphenated identity across multiple communities in America, Europe, and Africa and as a writer who navigated, like Hurston (and like Jemmy Button, William James, and both Langston Hughes and Katherine Dunham, as we will see in chapter 4), the tense colonial relationship of mentorship and patronage throughout his life. But while McKay's work has been lauded for its revolutionary impact on leaders of the Négritude movement from the (Martinican) Nardal sisters in Paris to Léopold Senghor in Senegal to Aimé Césaire in Martinique, it has also been criticized for this very grappling with multiple nodes of contact and affiliation: for his depiction of bifurcated alter egos superimposed on chaotic, teeming urban scenes or for the creation of characters who resolve their sense of psychic duality in a gesture of primitivizing essentialism that conflates them with the countryside. I invite a reading of McKay's characters, instead, as engaged in Hurston's strategic forms of ethnographic looking and of "feather-bed resistance," using these skills of observation and distancing to transition from the role of specimen to spectators. Through this strategic shift, we are also able to see how the protégé-patron encounter can be part of a vital protest tradition. This subtle resistance can also be mapped through many of the other encounters and readings in my work, from Hurston to the Christmas Day rebels, and to Jemmy Button himself, whose complicated navigation of cultural retentions and fluidities serve as strong rejoinders against any oversimplified accusation of primitivism, dualism, or essentialism their patrons, masters, or readers may have leveled against them.[74]

Claude McKay left his native Jamaica for the United States in August 1912, at the age of twenty-one, to study agronomy at Tuskegee. Leaving behind the supportive mentorship of his older brother, U'Theo, a local schoolteacher, and the financial and artistic patronage of English aristocrat-turned-amateur folklorist Walter Jekyll, McKay looked ahead to the tutelage of Booker T. Washington, whose accomplishments, "real and imaginary, obscured from McKay's distant gaze the hard realities" of race relations in the United States.[75] As biographer Wayne F. Cooper relates, "while the great black majority" in Jamaica "remained fated by poverty, illiteracy, and governmental neglect, they suffered few of the brutal denials of legal rights that characterized American race relations during this same period."[76] From formalized segregation to everyday acts of overt and insidious prejudice, U.S. racism "horrified" McKay: "My spirit revolted against the ignoble cruelty and blindness of it all."[77] His spirit was further dampened by the "semimilitary, machinelike existence" of life at Tuskegee, which emphasized discipline over intellectual rigor. Enamored though he remained with the commanding, charismatic personality of Booker T. Washington, McKay soon made plans to leave Tuskegee, transferring to Kansas State and then moving, after a two-year course there, to New York City. Although McKay wrote little of his time at Kansas, it is here that he gained early exposure to two radical philosophies that would shape the rest of his career: socialism and Du Boisian double consciousness.

But even as he raged against social inequalities in his poetry, and even as he began his slow reconciliation with his own double consciousness as the son of West Indians educated in the British imperial tradition, McKay continued to write about "'primitive' life in North Africa" in exchange for the checks he received from his U.S. patron, the same "Godmother" Charlotte Mason who supported Zora Neale Hurston, Langston Hughes, and other writers of the Harlem Renaissance as well.[78]

McKay's literary life was shaped by his vexed relationships with his mentors and patrons, starting with his earliest and most lasting relationship with Walter Jekyll, the British expatriate who sought refuge in rural Jamaica from the hypocrisies of both the British and the Jamaican elite. Jekyll took a keen interest in the young McKay, who happened to be working as an apprentice to a wheelwright when Jekyll stopped to have his carriage repaired. When he learned the nineteen-year-old McKay was actually an aspiring poet, Jekyll was immediately intrigued. He encouraged the young "peasant poet" to get back in touch with his "spontaneous" peasant culture by writing in dialect and rewarded him financially for doing so. It is ironic that McKay and Jekyll mirrored for each other a persona made possible by the very conflict they wished the other to resolve: McKay's interest in Jekyll was fueled, in part, by the young poet's exposure to nonconformist, anticolonial ideals, and a burgeoning ontology of exile that emerged from conversations he had with local schoolteachers and professionals at his brother's home. Jekyll's interest in McKay, on the other hand, was fueled by his own ontological ideal of the uncorrupted peasant. The ideal "peasantry" that Jekyll saw in McKay was, in reality, a convergence of his imperial education and a growing political investment in local struggles. The ideal "nonconformity" that McKay found in Jekyll was, in fact, a product of his aristocratic wealth and colonialist ideology of primitivism.[79]

This paradoxical cathexis brought inevitable tension between the two men, especially when McKay included poems about rebellion and protest in his work. As critics have noted, Jekyll "encouraged his protégé to censor any militancy" that might threaten Jekyll's own position in the community by exposing him as an interloper or colonial presence. Thus poems like McKay's early-acclaimed "George William Gordon to the Oppressed Natives"—in which the Morant Bay Rebels of 1865 are lauded for their protest—were never anthologized in his lifetime because of Jekyll's disapproval.[80]

Despite the strong influence of these patrons (Jekyll and Mason) at home and abroad, McKay continued to publish radical poetry and fiction and gained notoriety as he traveled throughout his life from the United States to Russia, England, Paris, and Morocco from 1919 to 1934. Leaders of the Négritude movement cited his writings as "having a galvanizing effect" on their own work in fostering a pan-African solidarity that rejected colonial influences in favor of African influences.[81] Léopold Senghor, in particular, felt aligned more literally with McKay's depiction of "the folk" in novels like *Banjo* (1929) and his protagonist's notion that "a black man even though educated was in closer biological kinship to the swell of primitive earth life."[82] But references to "the folk" in McKay's writings were most often retranslated, in French, as "the people," or "the proletariat," and critical excerpts from *Banjo* (in which Léopold Senghor also appears as a minor character) were often reprinted in radical Afro-Caribbean newspapers across France to illustrate McKay's indictment, in that work and others, of the colonial enterprise.[83] As Afro-Caribbean surrealist and communist Étienne Léro dramatically expressed, "the wind that blows from black America will soon manage . . . to cleanse our Antilles of the aborted fruit of an obsolete culture. Langston Hughes and Claude McKay, two revolutionary black poets, have brought us, marinated in red alcohol, the African love of life, the African joy of love, the African dream of death."[84]

McKay's reliance on bifurcated protagonists—the unlikely friendship between the urban drifter and returning G.I. Jake and the Haitian thinker, Ray, in *Home to Harlem* (1928), who reappears in a different setting, on the docks of Marseilles in *Banjo* (1929), where he meets the eponymous musician Banjo—has led to an easy critical interpretation of his work as committed to resolving the struggle between European and African influences. But my own reading, in bringing the larger critical frame of patronage to bear on McKay's work, insists that we examine these relationships and dualities in a less tidy way, as I have done throughout this chapter and this book, by interrogating the space between the specimen and the scientist, the observer and observed, the patron and the protégé. The tensions of this space are most clearly expressed—and in a manner most relevant to this project's larger lens of inquiry—in McKay's final novel, *Banana Bottom* (1933), and its complex navigation of double consciousness.

Critics have argued that McKay finally resolves the dualism of his earlier works, albeit in a troubling manner, with the fully integrated character of Bita Plant, the protagonist of his final novel who does what McKay never did after his departure from Jamaica in 1912—return home to her village, in this case (the fictional) Banana Bottom. *Banana Bottom* offers its own take on the problem of patronage, creating a series of overlapping binaries throughout the text, most of which involve the protagonist herself positioned against different mentoring characters as foils: In the three major ones, first, the self-assured but too-young Bita is juxtaposed with the eccentric, older, mixed-race Crazy Bow; then, the native-return Bita is paired with the expatriate Squire Gensir (modeled after Jekyll himself); and finally, the novel's primary tension mounts by pitting the free-spirited, educated, increasingly agnostic Bita against her strict, missionary pedagogue, Priscilla Craig.

Some critics read Bita as a heroic character who embodies an "alternative folk modernity" closely aligned with a Senghorian sensibility of folk art as vital to the staging of social protest. They also read her as one who embodies, through her eventual marriage to the drayman and peasant Jubban, the economic sensibility of a Jamaican peasantry poised "to take advantage of the remains of the plantation system" in order to "accumulate their own property" and cultivate their own lands. If we read the story of Bita and Banana Bottom within this larger context, explains critic David Nicholls, "we can see peasant life as a form of resistance to British colonial rule and a significant staking out of economic autonomy."[85] Yet others insist that such a heroic reading of the hemmed-in Bita ignores the essentialist, overly feminized primitivism of McKay's resolution, one that continues to nostalgize and romanticize peasant life and that clips the wings of the intellectually and creatively gifted Bita, relegating her to a passive, antifeminist, naturalist silence. But these readings that either exalt the work as McKay's triumphant resolution of psychic duality or dismiss it as yet another example of pandering primitivism do not account for the multilayered shifts in Bita's relationships and within her own character.[86]

In order to redeem Bita's character as a strong and significant portrayal of African-Atlantic personhood, we must look more closely, as Robert Young has argued, at "the commerce between cultures."[87] Critic Paul Jay rightly takes up Young's interest in heterogeneity and cultural interchange in his own reading of McKay's work and calls further on Gilroy's reading of the "rhizomorphic, fractal structure of the transcultural, international formation" as one way to understand Bita's position as *neither* African *nor* English *nor* Jamaican but as a young woman who navigates a Black Atlantic consciousness that occupies the "space between."[88] But while Jay still finds that McKay's "critique of absolutist discourse" is often infected and reinforced by the very ideology it seeks to replace," I contend that McKay offers a subtle mockery of this ideology by turning the lens of observation on watchers like Squire Gensir himself and empowering Bita with her own performative and introspective lens as she envisions for herself and for readers what Gensir's final days may have been like upon *his* own native-return journey back to England—a vision of imperial return that exists only in Bita's pitying imagination of the aging, helpless man forced to return "home."[89]

Within the context of my own larger project, I invite a new reading of McKay's final novel, as it echoes and bookends the journeys I have tracked so far, featuring a Bhabhian mimic-woman who returns from a forced educational and religious mission abroad with renewed fervor for her native homeland (like Jemmy Button), and who is also forced to reconcile with the power of imperial influence in shaping her renewed vision of her old life. This imperial influence, in turn, is not just reflected in the missionary presence of Priscilla and the Reverend Malcolm Craig but is more keenly mirrored for Bita in the persona of Squire Gensir, the transcultural outcast who assimilates (like Franz Boas, and like Jekyll, too) to his adoptive homeland(s). McKay's twentieth-century variation of this "native return" narrative, and the productive complications evoked by his protagonist, Bita Plant, turn my project's lens more fully to the twentieth century and the work of ethnography in unmooring personhood from the strict logic of self-possession and affiliation to an understanding of it as a performative, accumulating, and necessarily destabilizing act.

McKay's novel begins with the much-anticipated return of the young Bita Plant to her rural village of Banana Bottom after seven years of missionary tutelage in the Mother Country with the Reverend Malcolm and Mrs. Priscilla Craig. While the circumstances that necessitate Bita Plant's departure are very different from the impromptu kidnapping of Jemmy Button, her subsequent return and abandonment of the Mission invite interesting comparisons that deepen our insights into the act of reencounter and the politics of transculturation and personhood.

Bita is sent away at thirteen, after an observant relative determines that she has had sex with the eccentric musical genius Crazy Bow, a descendant of the colonial aristocracy whose Scottish grandfather freed all of his slaves and then married "one of the blackest of them."[90] Crazy Bow "was the colour of a ripe banana" and ten years senior to Bita (4). Although Bita's father, the villagers, and the Craigs treat this incident as a rape (and rightly so, considering the vast difference in age and the inability of either the young Bita or the teched Crazy Bow to articulate and register consent), readers are, in fact, encouraged to read this peculiar scene as an introduction to Bita's independence and self-possession. Bita is introduced, even in flashback, as a confident young girl from the start of the novel. She is pleased by the friendship and eventual flirtatious power she asserts over Crazy Bow, even as she learns from him the power of music and artistic expression. From the start, we are shown the ways in which Bita has a more complicated and mature understanding of the relationship between mentor and protégé as a relationship of reciprocal power and exchange.

While most of the children in the village feared Crazy Bow, Bita did not, choosing to go with her father to listen to this "coloured Paganini" play, often meeting him by the riverside when she went to gather mangoes, and eventually becoming his regular companion. Once, in one of their many romps through the fox-tail grass, "Bita got upon Crazy Bow's breast and began rubbing her head against his face." Crazy Bow resists her, pushing her away "rather roughly," opting instead to play her a sweet love song upon his fiddle. Bita listens, posing "in the attitude of a bewitched being," and as soon as he finished, "she clambered upon him again and began kissing his face." He fends her off for as long as he can, but "blinded by temptation," he finally succumbs, "and the deed was done" (9–10).

And so, the narrator writes of Bita's predicament, in a deliberately dramatic tone: "Before she was thirteen she had fallen into the profound pit that yawned between the plane of the peasantry and higher achievement." The narrator then waxes on, turning Bita into a metonym for the missionary (read: racist) vision of Jamaica itself, in a seemingly tongue-in-cheek soliloquy: "Young Africa, expatriate, emancipated, turning out of barracoons and huts, pressing forward, eager eyes fixed upon the Light held high by a white hand, tripping and falling ingloriously in the sweet snare of the flesh" (15). This long tribute continues, reading almost like stage directions for the introduction of Priscilla Craig, who enters the scene soon after, with her "generations of Northern training in reserve, restraint and Christian righteousness," stepping in to save "poor Bita" from this yawning gulf, whisking her away to England for "seven years' sound education," while Crazy Bow is whisked away to the madhouse (31).

It is in a more subdued moment of postlapsarian return that we, in fact, first meet Bita in the present, after her seven-year sojourn abroad, now playing at the Mission house in Jubilee. Once a protégée of the musical Crazy Bow, the novel opens with *her* musical performance, as she plays "the old straight piano to the singing of the Coloured Choristers in the beflowered school-room." Bita's debut is introduced to readers as "the most exciting [Sunday] in the history of Jubilee." The first in her village to be educated abroad, Bita is now "a real young lady wearing a long princess gown and her hair fixed up in style," preparing to return to her home village of Banana Bottom in a few days for Emancipation Day celebrations (1). Bita thus makes her reentry into native culture as a poised, intelligent, and beautiful young woman, or, from the Craigs' perspective "one precious flowering of a great work" (11).

The Craigs' patronage, in fact, has a far more repressive influence on Bita than the blurred relationship she had with Crazy Bow, in which the role of mentor and student was more fluid and organically unstable. The Craigs, instead, wield an exacting power on the young woman's behavior, movements, and associations. But here, once again, the self-possessed Bita bears neither resentment nor fear of reprimand when she speaks with pride about her hardworking people and the economic disparities that drive them to labor, for example, on the Panama Canal. When Priscilla Craig complains that "our Negroes are not the same after contact with the Americans. They come back ruder," Bita quickly retorts that "they make more money there, though. . . . They say the construction is mighty work and the black labour the best down there . . . especially the Jamaicans and Haitians." Bita also befriends the local peasants and gives in to the "surging big free feeling" she feels when she is "baptized" in the market at Jubilee, mingling for the first time in the crowd, responding, for the first time, to "the colour, the smell, the swell and press" of the market, that "gave her the sensation of a reservoir of familiar kindred humanity into which she had descended for baptism" (35, 41). It is here that Bita is reborn and reacclimated, though it is important to note her observation that "she had never had that big moving feeling as a girl when she visited the native market. And she thought that if she had never gone abroad for a period so long, from which she had become accustomed to viewing her native life in perspective, she might never had had that experience" (40).

The transformative power of contact with *her own people* is made palpable and articulable for Bita only through the act of defamiliarization— through contact with outsiders. Only after literalizing the diasporic experience through exile can Bita experience this rebirth at home, this baptismal purity of a communal, diasporic kinship. The missionary gesture, far from dissolving native ties and tendencies, serves instead to strengthen them, as happened with Jemmy Button, too. Empowered with a unique vision of the people, or "spyglass," to borrow Hurston's term for the ethnographic lens, Bita now occupies a unique space between spectacle and spectator. As one who has spent time under the scrutinizing spell of the imperial machine, Bita's return home is imbued, yes, with the nostalgia for a childhood ease and the longing for (a now unrealizable) surrender—these are, in some respects, typical of any *bildungsroman* or rite-of-passage tale. But along with this more typical yearning, Bita carries, through the experience of exile, a heightened sense of her position between cultures, and a newly awakened sense of responsibility and vision as one who is simultaneously a cultural outsider and insider.

Bita's final experience with patronage lies somewhere between Crazy Bow's pliability and the Craigs' rigidity (though both of those early relationships considerably altered her fate and shaped the person she has become at novel's opening). But her relationship with Squire Gensir is perhaps the most profound of the patron-protégé relationships in this novel and is the most clearly autobiographical part of the story for McKay. As revealed in McKay's dedication of the novel to the memory of "Pacjo" (the nickname bestowed upon Jekyll by the Jamaican peasantry), and in his Author's Note that relegates all characters to the realm of the imaginary, "perhaps except Squire Gensir," the relationship between Bita and the squire is based most directly on McKay's own relationship with Jekyll.

Bita's relationship with Squire Gensir is platonic, but as critic Rhonda Cobham has discussed, "the excesses of the sexual relations that hedge in the chaste minuet between Gensir and Bita . . . speak to the anxieties that belied McKay's posture of self-assurance in his own dealings with white patrons."[91] Indeed, by trading the homosocial tensions of his relationship with Jekyll for the heterosocial "dance" between Bita and Gensir, McKay is able to both offer a bolder illustration and to level a bolder critique at the manipulative nature of his own relationship with Jekyll.

In fact, I would argue that the prequel of Bita's literal rape at the hands of her first protégé, and her mandatory cultural and gender transformation (from Jamaican tomboy to genteel lady) at the hands of her second, already places her in a stronger position in her relationship with the squire. Gensir, despite his erudition, is in many ways, Crazy Bow in colonial garb. Like Crazy Bow, he, too, is a queer character who does not fit into a traditional masculine sensibility. Crazy Bow's musical genius and sturdy-yet-delicate finesse with a bow have not endowed him for the work of a hardy peasant, nor does his eccentric, reclusive nature promise success in either the marriage or labor market. Likewise, Squire Gensir's cultivated distance from his aristocratic colonial background has rendered him a recluse and an outsider in both England and Jamaica. Thus both men have either stepped away or been removed from communities that cannot quite make a place for them, and in that sense, Bita is as much a mirror for their outsiderliness as she is a foil for each of them. Bita, in this queered colonialist reading, does not stand as a symbol for the fertile, untrammeled soil of virgin territory waiting to be conquered and tilled (though this is just how Priscilla Craig reads her, which adds yet another complicated layer to McKay's hetero/homo-social re-renderings), but rather mirrors back to both men, a younger, freer version of themselves— Bita as the both/and, free to set the parameters of her multiple affiliations, graced with a social ease and openness that none of the others possess.

The act of contact, as the novel continually reminds us, is always a corrupting, penetrating force, but Bita's power rests in her ability to *look back* in a manner that empowers her. Her return to Jamaica, along with her return gaze, provide her with the dual weaponry that McKay did not have in his arsenal—the social *and* economic mobility to look *back* from a space of safety and belonging. McKay, in fact, began writing *Banana Bottom* while working as a subsistence farmer on an acre of farmland in Tangier, "growing potatoes, peas, carrots and turnips for sustenance and struggling to write the novel that would restore him to financial stability."[92] He began the novel after hearing of Jekyll's death in 1928 and learning that the patron who had catapulted and directed his career for so long had left the holdings of his vast library to another young man—a new protégé—to whom McKay angrily referred as an "ignorant" and "unworthy" peasant.[93] McKay never regained financial stability or the literary stature he enjoyed in the 1920s, as the Great Depression led to poor sales of both the novel and the short story collection *Gingertown* (1932) that preceded it. He reluctantly returned to the United States in 1934 and accepted work with the Federal Writers' Project while completing his autobiography, *A Long Way from Home* (1937).

Thus McKay's fictional recasting of his relationship with Jekyll via Bita and Gensir offers a fairly strong critique of white patronage and how this experience might actually empower (as actualized for Bita, if not for McKay until much later) the protégé with a keener understanding of the *work* of diasporic personhood in talking back to colonial power. McKay uses the "folk" guise of Gensir as the most transparent entry point into this critique. For while Gensir views himself as an amateur folklorist of Jamaican culture, he cannot help but refer to the cultural crossings between Europe, Africa, and the West Indies (a Jamaican hill country tune that may be a variant of Mozart; a European fable with African origins) as acts of "stealing" or "borrowing," a happy trespass that nonetheless implies the existence of discrete cultural traditions (124). Through examples like this (from his alleged aversion to the stifling effects of modern education to his primitivist understanding of freedom—critiques he can level precisely *because* of his educational, economic, and racial mobility, as Bita is quick to critique), McKay shows readers that despite his desire to "live among the people," Gensir still views cultures as distinct entities or, at best, as overlapping traditions that are superimposed upon each other. He thus continues, in his role as folklorist, to model the role of Western conqueror—an outsider who enters and discovers not shifting similarities but an essential difference that only he, with his specialized knowledge, can extract from its original "source" to create a link in the chain, or to borrow and "wear," like Boas's own forms of cultural borrowing and manipulations of Inuit customs.

Gensir's amateur ethnography thus adopts the traditional scientific gaze in this period that ethnographers like Hurston and Dunham sought to overturn. Bita, too, follows Hurston and Dunham, inverting and repossessing Gensir's way of looking. When they first meet, they are "mutually curious" about each other, again because of their mirrored status—she, as "a peasant girl" who had just returned "from his own country" with a unique "charm and refinement," and he, as one who "represented in himself by education and by birth the flowering of that culture she had been sent abroad to obtain" yet chose "to live in the hills among the peasants and enjoyed it" (81). But while Gensir simply observes the events of the tea-meeting they attend together, Bita cannot help but be moved by the music, dancing with abandon and letting "the memories of her tomboyish girlhood" rush over her. Later, she glances at Gensir "and wondered what he was thinking and feeling. Clearly he was enjoying the evening. But it was merely cerebral, she thought. Were the nerves and body cells not touched as hers?" (85–86).

Bita inverts this lens throughout the story, refusing the role of both passive spectator and spectacle. Even in scenes when she is *performing for* the squire and is moved by all he knows, she is yet reading him, fetishizing and "primitivizing" *his* whiteness in much the same way that Gensir and Craig do when they read *her* and her people as quintessentially other to themselves. As she practices the minuet from Mozart for him in one scene, for example, "all the time her head was full of the thought: How strange he is! How strange he is! No white person had ever touched her with such a feeling of otherworldliness as this man" (127).

But the difference in this reading and a colonialist reading of Bita that might rely on the same language, I believe, lies in her more expansive understanding of the word *otherworldliness*. For Gensir and the Craigs, *otherworldliness* intimates a space of essential difference: a set of customs one might observe, understand, and in the case of Gensir, even study and appreciate. But they belong to an elsewhere against which they view their own distinct cultural affiliation and belonging. Gensir's desire, after all, is to live *among* the peasants, not to live *as* a peasant. In fact, when he tries to romanticize this position, Bita quickly disabuses him of his fantasy. When Gensir romantically sighs, "I don't think I am as free as the peasants here in their daily life. . . . So free that they don't have any idea of words like freedom and restraint," Bita pushes back immediately, stating "I don't agree. . . . What freedom do they have? Plodding and digging and digging all day. . . . And you—you have had the run of the world. Even here, you can go anywhere from the governor's house to the lowest peasant's hut" (121).

Bita could as easily be scolding Boas here, for his own self-appointed license to move freely among the Inuit, manipulating his understanding of their hospitality customs to gain entry into their homes despite his knowledge of their discomfort with his presence there. As a result of whites' imperial "run of the world," enslaved and indigenous peoples have long had a keen understanding of the meanings of words like "freedom" and "restraint," as the history of rebellion by the Native Baptists and Morant Bay rebels in Jamaica highlight, and that the novel's early pairing of Emancipation Day as coincident with Bita's return makes clear. Such plaintive yearnings by Gensir thus highlight his basic ignorance of the politics of freedom in his adopted country.

When Bita realizes her preaching is falling on deaf ears, as Gensir continues on in a self-congratulatory manner about striking out on his own, she simply lets him wax on, asking him to "go on and tell me some more about yourself" (122). Bita knows, like McKay knew, like Hurston knew, like others before and since, that there is no *converting* the Gensirs and Craigs and Masons and Jekylls of the world to a new way of looking. Permeable as these parameters are, mere touristic or calculated exposure is not enough. A truly ethnographic and diasporic vision requires a conception and practice of personhood that actively resists an insistence on discrete parameters, one that emphasizes accumulation over distinction.

Although Bita is empathetic to *all* who have shaped her in some way, she retains her own independent voice, vision, and interpretive power both through and beyond these influences. As she remarks upon hearing Crazy Bow play the piano one evening after her return, "she was gripped by a deep sorrow that a human being, a rare artist, should be deprived of the ordinary faculties. . . . How bewitching was his playing! No wonder he had magnetized her into that trouble of his adolescence" (257). She grants that feminized power of "bewitchment" to Crazy Bow now, reminding us how she once *donned* the "attitude of a bewitched being" herself long ago, hinting that her power in this narrative and in this community has always been both transcultural, and also transgendered, controlling the terms as she does, of her own "bewitchment."

It is also important that Squire Gensir returns home to spend his final days in *his* native land at the end of the narrative, since he could not achieve the kind of transculturation in Jamaica that might have aided his growth and his anthropological endeavor. Once more, we are left with Bita's imagining of his "native return" and whether he "may have had some consolation dying among his own people. . . . He had seemed to her, after all, in spite of his free and easy contacts with the peasants, a lonely man living a lonely life. And although the peasants admired him, his high intelligence precluded him from sinking himself entirely in the austere simplicity of peasant life" (308–9).

While the surface of this narrative seems to insist on individuals maintaining a sense of pride in their "natural, unchangeable selves," Bita Plant's complex character and experiences elide and resist this simplistic reading. As she turns the ethnographic gaze on herself toward the end of the novel, undressing to admire her beautiful self in the mirror, she "thought of how the finest qualities of mind or brain or heart were the attributes of only the rarest spirits, who may spring like flowers in the commonest as much as the most exclusive places, in the proud domain as well as the peasant's lot and even in the hothouses. How then could any class or people or nation or race claim a monopoly of a thing so precious and so erratic in its manifestations?" (266). This literalization of diaspora—conjured for readers as she looks at her naked body in "the long mirror of the old-fashioned wardrobe," perhaps a mahogany relic of slave labor itself—brings together the novel's concerns with patronage as cultivation, and the diasporic, transcultural experience as a rejoinder to it. Bita Plant, in this moment of self-recognition, literalizes what she has been rehearsing throughout the text, through acts of Bhabhian mimicry, in which her appropriation of a British colonial model affords her a "double vision" that "disrupts" colonial authority. In this moment, Bita fully reverses the surveilling gaze that has shaped her life thus far, transforming it into the "displacing gaze of the disciplined, where the observer becomes the observed." By claiming *some* colonial power alongside diasporic power, Bita, like others throughout this project who engage in this double vision, "rearticulates the whole notion of identity and alienates it from essence."[94]

Through the story of Bita Plant, we are allowed, for the first time in this project, *inside* a story we have yet to experience only from the narratives of the watchers. Thus far, we have only witnessed the return of the native through the diaries of Darwin and FitzRoy, through the binoculars and hollers of shipboard captains along the shore, and through court transcripts, newspaper articles, and mission notes. Like Jemmy "Button," Bita Plant's name evokes her role in the system of exchange. Like the item of barter for which Jemmy's mother accidentally exchanged her son with FitzRoy, Bita's given surname pronounces her fated relationship to Jamaica and the land, as if she is a seed meant for planting only in native soil.

And yet, if we are to carry the logic of her naming a bit further, we might add that she is just a "bit" of plant, a single stalk, most likely, of the strong and sturdy banana plants that grow in her small village. While "bit" might initially suggest diminution, it also suggests, in the context of Bita's travel and her magnetic ability to captivate everyone she encounters, that she is, in a communal sense, a "bit" of each of us, a perennial plant, like the banana, that does not grow in a linear season of growth, nor from a seed, but from a rhizome, a bit of rootstock from which new shoots can grow at any time. We might read Bita, then, as cultivated by contact and return, just as those she influences are, in turn, nourished as well.

Thus Bita, with her new routed, internationalist perspective, like Jemmy, reclaims her name from its implied function as a passive commodity in the market of imperial exchange, in large part by performing the failure of the imperial missionary gesture. Bita's grafting in the soil is not set according to the terms mandated by the Craigs, her father, or even Gensir.[95] Instead, the novel invites us to think of her transplantation in different terms: as an offshoot that has been routed through other histories, journeys, and spaces, she will now join and contribute to a communal ecology—a growth that is precisely the opposite of the passive immobilization implied by "rootedness," and that is more fluid and undisciplined than self-possession.

For even as the narrative grafts Bita in the soil of Jamaica within conventional terms of marriage and family, she remains connected to her imperial education, if no longer through the direct influence of Gensir's patronage, then through the lot of land, the furnished home, and the small sum of money he leaves her—a redemption that McKay never received in his real-life relationship with Jekyll. McKay does *not* naturalize the roles of Bita and her husband, Jubban, instead treating their life choices as the deliberate outcomes of their training: Jubban accepts that his wife "should excel in the things to which she had been educated," and Bita, in turn, accepts that Jubban should excel "in the work to which he had been trained" (313). Thus the future of Jamaica's prosperity rests in his labor and her intellect (another instance of queering a conventional gender dynamic of the time), granting them an economic mobility that is routed not through consolidation, compromise, or determinism but through an unmooring of the self from the strictures of *natural* belonging.

As I move into the work of Langston Hughes and Katherine Dunham in the final chapter, and beyond to the conclusion, we will examine more closely the role of contact in these acts of unmooring and move closer to a broader, more theoretical understanding of personhood as a powerful performance not of self-possession but of *unbecoming*, in which acts of contact hasten a productive and radical undoing of the fiction of distinction, in which there is no true "self" to "creep in unconsciously" beyond the narrative self that must necessarily articulate these acts of immersion and dissolution as the meeting or conjoining of distinct entities. It is through this fictional construction of the narrative "I" that Dunham, Hughes, and the other watchers we have followed throughout this work, help us, in our final turn, relinquish the fiction of self-possession altogether.

4

Performing Diaspora

The Science of Speaking for Haiti

The Caribbean is nothing but contact.
> Michel-Rolph Trouillot, "The Caribbean Region:
> An Open Frontier in Anthropological Theory"

> The god of the white man calls him to commit crimes; our god asks only good works of us. But this god who is so good orders revenge! He will direct our hands; he will aid us. Throw away the image of the god of the whites who thirsts for our tears and listen to the voice of liberty that speaks in the hearts of all of us.[1]

With these powerful words, delivered on a stormy August evening in 1791, a young religious leader and coachman named Boukman, originally from Jamaica, is said to have inspired a group of slaves in the Caïman woods of northern Saint-Domingue to raise arms against their French masters, igniting a revolutionary spark that would eventually lead to the birth of the nation of Haiti—the world's first independent black republic—in 1804.

Boukman, so named because he was a literate *man* of the *book* (not the Bible but the Qur'an), is described in various accounts of the infamous ceremony as officiating alongside a priestess "with strange eyes and bristling hair," or as Laurent Dubois writes, "a green-eyed woman of African and Corsican descent" named Cécile Fatiman.[2] There were—according to the only (and highly primitivized) account of Bois Caïman, written by Antoine Dalmas, who had served as a surgeon at the Gallifet plantation and survived the insurrection—blood oaths, ritual dances, rousing speeches, and the slaughter of a sacrificial pig. There were men and women of African and Creole descent, from coffee and sugar plantations all across the region—fieldworkers and overseers as culturally, economically, and religiously diverse as the rituals they performed and the priest and priestess who led them. While Dalmas's original account intended to discredit the revolution by highlighting the "barbarism" of this event, it was nevertheless soon taken up by abolitionists and Haitian writers and reconfigured to convey the drama, courage, and poetry of the ceremony. These writers added details to the account that have since become canonical, like the "dark and stormy" night, the text and attribution of the now-famous speech to the heroic Boukman, and the "oath" taken during the ceremony.[3]

The continued lure of this foundational myth for Haiti (for, again, it is unclear how much of it is truth or embellishment: Was the religious ceremony a grand pretext for surreptitious strategizing and arms distribution? Was it a staged distraction? Or was it a genuine marriage of religious and military fervor—the proclamation of a divine right to murder in the name of one's true god or gods?) appears to lie not in its remarkable display of cultural heterogeneity but, rather, in its purported aim of national unification. As scholars like Susan Buck-Morss have argued, the various interpretations of the Bois Caïman myth all tend to organize around or against the European story: Bois Caïman is either conjured as proof that Haiti had "entered into modernity proper because it joined the European story, the only story that counts," or used to indicate that Haiti had surpassed the European story. In either case, the myth has generally been used by scholars to mark the moment Haiti officially became a nation, "complete with its own . . . pedigree of 'founding fathers,' and a bloody birth through the sovereign sacrifice of human life."[4]

Scientific and cultural accounts added to the chorus, as ethnographies of Haiti after the revolution and well into the twentieth century employed a similar unifying gesture. However, these accounts looked to a different consolidating force: If Haiti was thought by some to have joined the European story after the revolution, others sought to recuperate the African story embedded in Haiti. Travel writer and exoticizer extraordinaire William Seabrook, for example, wrote famously and problematically in his 1929 *The Magic Island* of the essential Africanism he found running through the "soul" of Haiti: "Something more than atavistic savagery, but which may trace none the less to their ancestral Africa, dark mother of mysteries—some quality surges to the surface of group or individual; and when this happens, we others are in the presence of a thing shorn of all that can provoke superior smiles or scorn, a thing which strikes terror and sometimes awe."[5]

American ethnographer Melville Herskovits also saw these essential Africanisms in the heart of Haitian culture. After extensive fieldwork throughout Africa and the Caribbean in the 1920s and 1930s, and despite his understanding that Haitian civilization was "the result of close and continued" contact between Europeans and Africans, he nevertheless held to the belief that these peoples and traditions were utterly dissimilar. Instead of a New World interculture, Herskovits primarily saw the remnants of Africa: "The presence of members of native ruling houses and priests and diviners among the slaves," he writes, "made it possible for the cultural lifeblood to coagulate through reinterpretation instead of ebbing away into the pool of European culture." While he does account for a process of "acculturation" that "resulted in varied degrees of reinterpretation of African custom" in light of "new situations," Herskovits sees in Haiti the emergence of "full-blown African civilizations" rather than the reflection of European or New World communities. It is Africa, not the Afro-Caribbean, he sees in these "independent or quasi-independent Negro communities."[6]

But for members of the African diaspora on American shores, the Haitian Revolution had long told a more expansive and diffuse story. Indeed, for U.S. African Americans like Frederick Douglass, Haiti was held up as an exemplary model of liberty, as "the original pioneer emancipator of the nineteenth century" that inspired other countries in the defeat of slavery on their own shores. Speaking at the Haitian Pavilion at the Chicago World's Fair in 1893, Douglass told his audience that "the freedom you and I enjoy today; the freedom that eight hundred thousand colored people enjoy in the British West Indies; the freedom that has come to the colored race the world over, is largely due to the brave stand taken by the black sons of Haiti nearly ninety years ago."[7] But Douglass's vision of Haiti extended beyond the European story of nationalism, beyond the terrestrial roots of the Americas and Europe. Douglass understood that the "roots" of this tree of liberty, as Haiti's own founding father, Toussaint Louverture, had famously stated at the time of his surrender, "are deep and numerous" and extended beyond the borders of the nascent nation and the sea that surrounded it.[8] Douglass reminded his audience of this, stating that when Haitians "struck for freedom, they builded better than they knew. Their swords were not drawn and could not be drawn simply for themselves alone. They were linked and interlinked with their race, and striking for their freedom, they struck for the freedom of every black man in the world."[9]

Haiti, as "the greatest of all our modern teachers," then, stood for something far more profound than just a political mirror for European models of nationalism, as more than just a warning signal to slaveholding interests in the United States, and as more than just a cultural mirror of Africa.[10] Haiti's roots, like other spaces in the Americas, were a complex web of Arawak, Creole, African, and European cultural and political traditions. As scholars from Edward Said to Jonathan Scott have discussed, the voice of Haiti's New World nationalism, keenly performed in C. L. R. James's 1938 *Black Jacobins*, "bridges an important cultural and political gap between Caribbean, specifically black, history on the one hand, and European history on the other. Yet it . . . is fed by more currents and flows in a wider stream than even its rich narrative may suggest."[11]

The birth of Haiti, as the name itself performed, was the birth of a cultural and political space that stood simultaneously for the indigenous and the foreign—for rootedness and diffusion. Unlike a United States culture that flattened racial and class distinctions in the service of "successful" nationalism, Haiti stood as a bold counterexample for the New World, in which traditional models of nationalism and imperialism had been supplanted in its very emergence.

In fact, a complex interplay between the indigenous, the African, and the European was part of Haiti's successful military strategy during the revolution. As historian Brenda Plummer discusses, "black resistance retained a specifically indigenous character, in spite of the innovations that the *philosophe* and the French Revolution made possible."[12] This points to the "eclectic sources of Haitian politics and thought," as Haitian state formation "originated in circumstances both cosmopolitan and local." She explains how the struggles between the African and Creole fighters during the revolution actually led to a unique collaboration of indigenous and European strategies in fighting the colonial forces: "African guerillas' strength lay in their tactical flexibility; their capacity to use Vodun as a psychological weapon; and the solidarity created by close ethnic ties in isolated communities." Later, when the Westernized Creoles joined the fight, they "brought to the anticolonial movement a battle-tested knowledge of modern military science and the rudiments of political organization."[13]

Even after the revolution, as Haitians sought to define and unify their national identity, they did not rely on static concepts of citizenship borrowed from the United States or France. Instead, as Plummer explains, they "proclaimed themselves *noirs*—'blacks,'" and admitted to this category "any Indians or mulattoes who considered themselves Haitians. Even renegade Polish mercenaries, stranded in Haiti after the expulsion of the French army, shared this attribute."[14]

While Haiti's founding myth cannot entirely escape the clutches of European tradition and interpretation, and while some ethnographic interventions are intent on situating Haiti's origins in Africa, Haiti's origin story, in fact, deliberately resists genealogy, for it is, in a Deleuzian sense, a story of becomings and undoings—of movement and change.[15] Its dramatic shifts, from indigenous Arawak community to European colony, from transatlantic slavery to global sovereignty, are better viewed through a panoramic lens that envisions Haiti as part of the larger Caribbean archipelago and beyond. A more fully realized understanding of Haiti, its history, and its troubled present, then, requires an extraction—or perhaps the proper word, to borrow from Caribbean intellectual Édouard Glissant, would be *diffraction*—from the limiting, disciplining myths of nation and land, to a more expansive view of its position as an "island bridge," as Antonio Benítez-Rojo has called it, between North and South America.[16]

For the Haitian experience, as Buck-Morss has argued, "was not a modern phenomenon, *too*, but *first*," and it is well worth considering whether its unique strides toward becoming a postcolonial, postslavery society were flatly incommensurate with the fictional promise of a European-inspired model of nationhood—but *not* because Haitian society and its leadership were socially unprepared or politically immature. Rather, Haiti betrayed the fissures in the existing rhetoric of nationalism by virtue of its *advanced* position in the economics of modernity, its leaders' open-eyed understanding of the role of labor and servitude in that economic process, and its constitutional interculture, from linguistic creolization to religious syncretism. In other words, Haiti is not an example of failed nationalism, but, rather, Haiti *exposes* the failures within the disciplinary model of nationalism itself.[17]

In this chapter, I build on the rereadings of the Caribbean offered by Atlantic world scholars like Glissant, Gilroy, Dubois, C. L. R. James, and others, and turn to U.S. African Americans Katherine Dunham and Langston Hughes, each of whom traveled there in the new century to "study" and compare the Haitian diasporic experience with their own. As other(ed) U.S. citizens, in their overlapping capacities as artists, ethnographers, and diasporic, postcolonial kin, these writers emphasize the centrality of *performance* in what Antonio Benítez-Rojo calls the culture of the "meta-archipelago"—"a chaos that returns, a detour without a purpose, a continual flow of paradoxes."[18] Performance effectively and constitutionally resists both isolationism and the neocolonial presence, for it is an act that, through both its ephemerality and acute awareness of scrutiny, reveals a culture in flux. Thus for Dunham and Hughes, Haiti and the other Antillean islands are no longer depicted as the lagging stepchildren of modernity but are offered, instead, as stunning exemplars of a burgeoning postmodernity— the earliest representatives of an open-ended, global network that is best understood as a "meta-archipelago," with neither boundaries nor a center but an outward diffusion that "takes away the space that separates the onlooker from the participant."[19] Haiti is reinvigorated through such readings and their emphasis on the distinctively "aquatic" aspect of Caribbean cultures, "the natural and indispensable realm of marine currents, of waves, of folds and double-folds, of fluidity and sinuosity."[20]

It is easy to lose track of the political valence of an argument so steeped in poetic re-renderings of Antillean space. No doubt, the visual image of this archipelago as an unlikely but powerful bridge, emerging in a vast sea to connect the routes and histories of multiple peoples of the world, is a compelling redemption and acknowledgment of its vital power for the modern West, and a necessary redress to the narratives of conquest and domination that have overshadowed the histories of survival, adaptation, and profound cultural influences on all sides of its oceanic borders. But my desire to reintroduce Haiti as a space that challenges the political and geographic borders of "nation" is not intended as a utopian rescue that erases or diminishes its continuing political, social, and economic struggles. Rather, it is offered as a productively problematic counterreading of "nation" itself as performance, with borders measured not by finite shorelines that divide land and sea but through cultural crossings between persons and across oceans.

Ethnography, once understood to be a discipline closely linked to the imperial enterprise, today may be considered the discipline that engages most directly with this idea of nation as cultural performance. In fact, the subgenre of performance ethnography, studied and employed by scholars and practitioners like Diana Taylor, Richard Schechner, and others, examines cultures and nations within the framework of mobility and contact.[21]

Yet to refer to performance ethnography as a kind of subgenre is, in effect, an act of redundancy in itself, since all ethnography is exemplary of what performance theorist Richard Schechner has called "twice-behaved behavior."[22] It is the continuous reiteration of cultures in motion that renders impossible the search for cultural origin or cultural purity.

This chapter is, in effect, a backward glance at the entire cultural-historic period of this study, as it begins (via the 1791 revolt) with a pre-Darwinian, protonational look at the Atlantic world and traces the impact of ethno-scientific narratives on the political and artistic performances—resistant or celebratory—of nationhood into the mid-twentieth century. Haiti encompasses all of the threads I have attempted to unravel in this book—from racial and cultural hybridities that cannot be subsumed under the umbrella of a singular nationalism, to the peculiar role of science in calling attention to the inevitability of these crossings that had been going on, in practice, for centuries before scientific interpellation (with all its own myriad crossings) articulated them.

In the elaboration that follows, I will examine nineteenth- and twentieth-century anxieties surrounding the birth and progression of Haiti as a nation in flux. I will move from a brief historical trajectory of the region that engages these anxieties, into the readings of Haiti's cultural and political impact on U.S. understandings of race through the works of artist-ethnographers who traveled to the region and were politically and culturally transformed by their experiences.

From primitivist imaginings of Haiti rendered by twentieth-century artists and ethnographers like Eugene O'Neill and Melville Herskovits, I move to Katherine Dunham's 1936 journey to Haiti, which solidified her already-blossoming career as a pioneering dance choreographer and led to the eventual publication of her 1969 ethnographic memoir, *Island Possessed*. In this work, Dunham depicts with honesty and vulnerability the blurring of lines between participant and observer, scientist and artist, and perhaps most compellingly, the duality of her position as "invader" and community member. I close my analysis with Langston Hughes's excursion to Haiti, which was a vacationer's sojourn turned political awakening. His political radicalization and eventual rewriting of Haiti's origin myth is a compelling testament to the transatlantic solidarity I wish to trace through this chapter.

I engage primarily with the work of these two U.S.-based artist-ethnographers precisely because of their outsider status—not only as non-Haitians but as cultural outsiders from the U.S. national frame. These writers were compelled not only by the story of Haiti's exile from the international political realm but by the lure of its history, and the journeys of its people, which held a mirror to their own. Immersed in the cultural productivity of the Harlem Renaissance and often brought together by their mutual creative interest in the stage and a shared frustration with the limits of the 1930s New Deal–sponsored Federal Theatre Project (which often refused to fund their most daring work, including Hughes's *Troubled Island*, which I take up later in this chapter), these two artist-ethnographers shared a particular bond in their desire to suture science, art, and politics in their work.[23]

Both Dunham and Hughes experienced more than just a surface defamiliarization in their journeys to Haiti. They came back emboldened to link the Haitian experience to U.S. concerns at home. Where some may have come home to advocate U.S. exceptionalism, Hughes and Dunham instead came home and advocated inter-American continuities. The two collaborated in writing and stage productions on various occasions throughout their long careers, including Hughes's completion of the jacket notes for a recording called *Song of Haiti*, by Haitian singer Jean Vincent, who had performed with Dunham's dance troupe.[24]

What I hope to emphasize in my own analysis, and what I think these U.S. narratives about Haiti—and perhaps, more broadly, of the Caribbean at large—so richly exemplify, is the complex interplay between science and art, where the impossibility of objectivity and authenticity (racial, cultural, political) finally come to light, and performance reveals itself as the only available, albeit temporary, truth. This, I think, is one of the most profound lessons that nineteenth-century science articulated to the modern West and that transatlantic interculture had been rehearsing for centuries.

A sustained look at Haiti through the lens of these artist-ethnographers who traveled back and forth across the island bridge provides new insight into the linkages between Haiti, the United States, and the solidarity that exists across diasporic groups and spaces. While Haiti has long been burdened with an exceptional status in American politics and anthropological study as a "grotesquely unique" space, the intervention of artist-ethnographers like Dunham and Hughes brings Haiti into focus as foundational to the prosperity of a powerful, global, diasporic solidarity—no longer a solitary, exceptional example but a vital link in a continuous chain of uprisings and uplift.[25] For in Haiti's struggles are mirrored the struggles of a global diasporic community whose very foundations rest and crack on questions of racial identity and performance. Ethnography, as a methodology, allows its practitioners to highlight this more seamlessly than other disciplines, and the artist-ethnographers featured here had a particular understanding of this fact. As U.S. African Americans, these scholar-artists navigated the everyday "ironies and complicities"